sweetly stitched
HANDMADES

AMY SINIBALDI

Tuva Publishing
www.tuvayayincilik.com

Address: Merkez Mah. Cavusbasi Cad. No:71
Cekmekoy / Istanbul 34782 - TURKEY

Tel: +9 0216 642 62 62

Sweetly Stitched Handmades

First Print: 2014 / December, Istanbul

All Global Copyrights Belongs To
Tuva Tekstil San. ve Dış Tic. Ltd. Şti.

Content: Sewing

Editor in Chief: Ayhan DEMİRPEHLİVAN
Project Editor: Kader DEMİRPEHLİVAN
Designer: Amy SINIBALDI
Technical Advisor: K. Leyla ARAS
Graphic Design: Ömer ALP, Abdullah BAYRAKÇI
Photography: Amy SINIBALDI, Tuva Publishing
Assistant: Büşra ESER

ISBN: 978-605-5647-66-7

Printing House
Bilnet Matbaacılık ve Ambalaj San. A.Ş.
Dudullu Organize Sanayi Bölgesi 1. Cadde No:16
Ümraniye - Istanbul / TURKEY

 facebook.com/TuvaYayincilik

twitter.com/TuvaYayincilik

 pinterest.com/TuvaPublishing

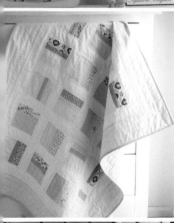

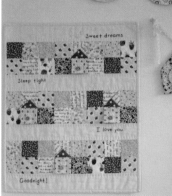

Table of Contents

introduction

I'm a self-taught sewer (that means a lot of trial and error!), so I love to encourage beginning sewers or even more advanced sewists to try new things. If I can do it, you can do it, I say. You see, my mother is a great cook and baker. Her realm is most definitely in the kitchen where she conjures up the best chocolate chip cookies anyone has ever tasted. As a child, she taught me how to sew a button if it fell off my jacket, but that was the extent of our sewing lessons. I learned how to use my first sewing machine, in 2006, by reading the instruction manual that came with it. I don't remember what made me think I could sew, but I do remember threading the machine for the first time (how intricate it seemed!) and being amazed that I was able to make it work. I started nanaCompany on Etsy soon thereafter and it's been a fantastic journey ~ from felt cookies and little girl aprons... to today.

So, this is my first book. I'm thrilled to pieces to get the chance to sew up these pretty little things and share them with you. I hope you are inspired by these projects and want to make them for yourself or someone you love. Better yet, one for you and one for someone you love.

In making handmade items, which requires oodles of time, care, and thought, you're already going above and beyond ~ and I commend you. In a world where most everything can easily be bought, and making anything by hand requires so much more effort, it thrills me to see all the beautiful handmades you're making.

I'm endlessly inspired by my crafty, quilty, bloggy friends ~ by what they're sewing today ~ but I'm also really inspired by those beautifully sewn handicrafts made by women hundreds of years ago. There is so much beauty in those quilts made completely by hand... the cross-stitch samplers... the rag dolls. I adore how imperfect and charming they are.

You might keep that spirit in mind while sewing with this book. Imperfections add charm. Character. Fight your perfectionist side. Fight the fear that's keeping you from simply beginning your next sewing project ~ because of an intimidating technique, or an untried method. Have fun and enjoy the learning process that each project brings. And always, always, keep creating!

xo amy

9

my favorite tools

Besides the basics ~ good scissors, iron, seam ripper, rotary cutter, self-healing cutting mat, quilting rulers, needles and thread ~ I find myself always reaching for these handy tools. Frixion pens by Pilot are so cool, you can write on your fabric and remove the ink with a touch of hot iron.

❀ Fabric glue stick. Truly one of my best friends. It's water soluble, a dab is all you need, and no messing with sharp pins.

❀ Mountain Mist Cream Rose 100% cotton batting. This batting is silky and on the thin side, which means it will drape well ~ that's what I love about it. It's perfect for the temperate climate in southern California. Also it is recommended for those who do a lot of hand-sewing because it contains no scrim.

❀ Quilter's basting spray. This spray adheres your smaller quilt sandwiches together as well as pins, but without the hassle of pins. Love this stuff. So much better than pinning.

❀ For general quilting, I use Perle cotton floss No. 12 or 8 in white.

❀ Pellon Wonder Under is my favorite paper-backed fusible web.

❀ I love my Clover seam ripper. For the longest time I was using a freebie that came with my old sewing machine and I had no idea how bad it was. It makes a world of difference to use a good seam ripper!

❀ Sulky Sticky Fabri-Solvy. This is the tool you will absolutely need for transferring those tiny embroidery designs onto tricky linen.

❀ Non-slip quilting rulers.

❀ Clover hera marker. I use it to mark quilting lines and it's perfect because it doesn't leave any marks on the fabric.

my favorite patch

It's the little things that often make a big difference, and I've fallen in love with one such detail that always seems to bring just the right amount of charm to my handmade projects. For me, a small embroidered patch of linen does just that. I have included a design for each linen patch designated to a project in this book, however, these are only suggestions and I hope you'll have fun personalizing your patches however you like.

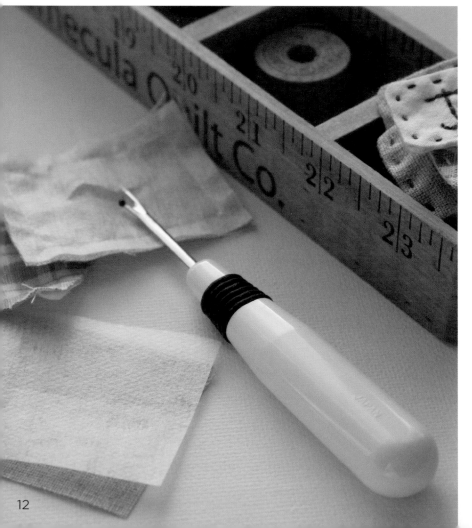

TO MAKE A PATCH

❀ Cut your desired shape (rectangle, square, circle, oval) + an extra ¼" (0.6cm) seam allowance on all sides from a piece of linen.Cut a duplicate from lightweight interfacing (the non-fusible kind).

❀ With right sides facing, sew a ¼" (0.6cm) seam around all edges, overlapping a few stitches at the beginning/end.

❀ Next, using a seam ripper, make a small slit in the center of the interfacing.

❀ Turn your shape right side out, ease out all the corners and press.

❀ Embroider your patch as you like.

❀ Sew it on by hand or machine to your project. I like to sew mine on by hand using a blind stitch.

tips

❀ No need to worry about the condition of the interfacing at the backside, or even if it rips all the way to the seam. It will not affect your patch and won't be seen once it's sewn into place. The stitches you use to attach the patch will maintain its shape.

❀ In general, I do not clip the corners of my patches because in most cases I prefer a rounded corner rather than a perfectly squared off edge.

❀ For me, the more imperfect the patch, the more charming. Have fun!

❀ To best achieve the look of ink in my embroidery (especially when embroidering words), I use two strands of black thread instead of embroidery floss.

❀ If you are using a lighter fabric, I suggest tracing your embroidery pattern on first, before you've made the patch. If you are using natural linen and find the patterns are difficult to trace, the best method I have found is tracing your pattern onto self-adhesive, water soluble, fabric like stabilizer (Sulky makes a good one) and sticking it right onto the linen, after the patch has been made. Stitch right through stabilizer and linen patch. Follow the instructions to remove the stabilizer. This is a great way to transfer any embroidery pattern to a difficult or dark fabric.

baby bear rattle

A handmade baby gift will always stand out among the piles of presents a new mom receives. Charming and sweet, this baby bear rattle is extra special when it's stuffed with a jingle ball (you can find these online or at your local craft store.) Gift the rattle on its own or coordinate your fabrics and pair it with a Ruffle Collar Baby Bib (see page 26) to make a perfect gift set.

Finished Size
4" x 7 ½"
10.2 x 19.1 cm

You will Need

- Two rectangles of blue ticking fabric 2 ½" x 3 ½" (6.4 x 8.9cm) for the handle
- Two rectangles of dotted fabric 2 ½" x 2" (6.4 x 5.1cm) for the handle
- One square of dotted fabric 2" (5.1cm) for the handle bottom
- Four squares of fabric 5" (12.7cm) for bear head
- Four squares of fabric 1 ¾" (4.4cm) for bear ears
- Two pieces of crochet trim 2 ½" (6.4cm) in length (5" total) (12.7cm total) for the handle
- One scrap of brown or black felt 1" (2.5cm) for Bear's eyes and nose
- One square of linen 2" (5.1 cm) for Bear's snout
- One square of lightweight interfacing 2" (5.1 cm) for Bear's snout
- Bear templates
- Cardstock or cereal box or cardboard for making patterns
- Brown embroidery floss (DMC 3031)
- Black thread
- Polyfill
- Jingle ball or rattle

INSTRUCTIONS

1 Copy the bear templates and create patterns using cardstock or other thin cardboard.

2 Position the bear head pattern diagonally onto the wrong side of a 5″ (12.7cm) square of fabric, and trace. It is placed diagonally so that the curved lines of the bear's head are cut on the fabric bias. Using another 5″ (12.7cm) square, cut a second head-piece in the exact same manner. Now flip the pattern over and cut two more head pieces on the bias of the remaining 5″ (12.7cm) squares.

3 Pair up one set of bear head fabric pieces so that they match up on all sides, right sides facing. Pair up the other set, right sides facing. Sew along the long smooth edge, backstitching at beginning and end. Repeat on second set. Clip the fabric seam allowance around the curve. Press the head-piece open with seam facing to one side. Repeat for second head-piece, pressing the seam to the same side, so when facing, the seams butt together.

4 Trace the bear's ear pattern to the wrong side of two pieces of ear fabric. Place two remaining pieces of ear fabric on these, right sides facing. Stitch the ears following your traced line. Trim the seam allowance and clip curves well. Turn ears right side out and press. Embroider a running stitch around the ear's edge using brown floss. Tip: Gently pull on the running stitch until the ear begins to curve in slightly.

5 Pin each ear 1″ (2.5cm) from the center seam of one head-piece, raw edges aligned, right sides facing. Machine-baste in place.

6 Machine-baste a length of crochet trim across the short side of a blue ticking rectangle, raw edges aligned. Repeat on second set.

7 With right sides facing, sew dot fabric to bottom of blue ticking fabric. Repeat for second piece. Press seams toward the dot fabric.

8 With right sides facing, sew the handle piece (along the crochet-trimmed edge) to the bottom straight edge of a bear head-piece. Repeat with second set. Press the seam towards bear head.

9 Lay rattle front and rattle back pieces together, right sides facing and pin at seams to make sure they line up.

10 Leaving the bottom of rattle open for turning right side out, stitch a 1/4″ (0.6cm) seam around the rattle (I stitched twice), then clip all curves, especially where the bear's head meets the handle. Turn right side out. Stuff well with polyfill, adding the jingle ball to the middle of bear's head. You'll find the head is quite shapeable ~ once I finished stuffing it, I added one last ball of stuffing precisely in the mouth area to achieve the look I wanted.

11 Fold the bottom edge of the rattle to the inside ¼" (0.6cm), and using a double strand of thread, sew a running stitch through this fold. Pull the thread until the hole in the bottom is as small as possible and knot thread. Trace the handle bottom pattern onto the dot fabric and cut out. Folding under a ¼" (0.6cm) as you go, stitch by hand to bottom of rattle.

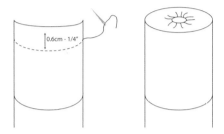

12 To make the bear's snout, trace the snout pattern onto linen. Sew onto the lightweight interfacing piece and trim the seam allowance. Using a seam ripper, carefully cut a slit into the interfacing, turn snout piece right side out and press. Using the brown floss, embroider a running stitch around the snout. Applique the snout by hand to bear head.

13 Cut the bear's eyes and nose from felt using the template. Stitch these onto the bears face, as pictured, using black thread and hiding the thread tails inside bear's head.

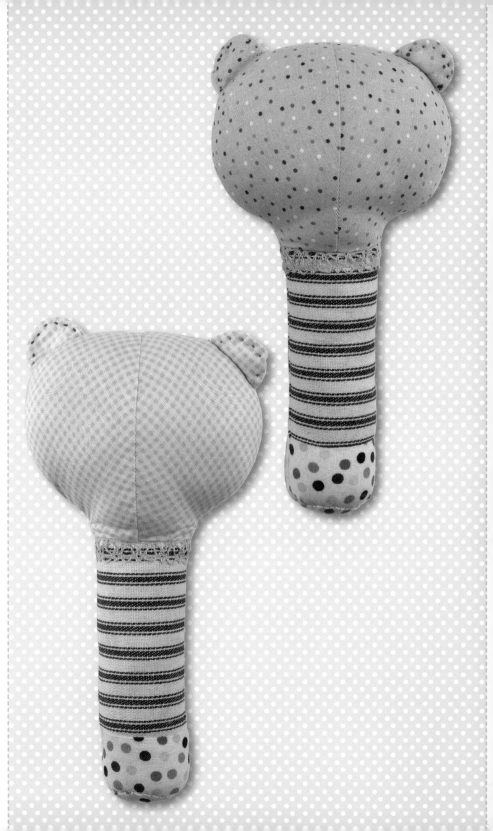

modern color block quilt

Have you discovered how fun it can be to sew with solids?   Maybe you already love it, but in the past I've always thought solids were too boring ~ now I'm totally hooked. What I love best is how solids make your printed fabrics really pop. For this quilt, each block consists of two complementary solids with just a sliver of print. I love the end result. And this quilt is perfectly sized for snuggling baby.

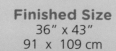

Finished Size
36" x 43"
91 x 109 cm

You will Need

- Twenty rectangles of assorted cotton solids 3" x 5" (7.6 x 12.7cm) for quilt blocks
- Twenty rectangles of assorted cotton solids 1 ¼" x 5" (3.2 x 12.7cm) for middle of quilt blocks
- Twenty rectangles of assorted cotton prints 1 ¾" x 5" (4.4 x 12.7cm) for quilt blocks
- Half-yard of white or off-white solid for 2 ½" (6.4cm) sashing strips
    - Cut fifteen 5" x 2 ½" (12.7 x 6.4cm) strips
    - Cut six 25" x 2 ½" (64 x 6.4cm) strips
    - Cut two 35" x 2 ½" strips (89 x 6.4cm)
- Half-yard of cotton solid for 4 ½" (11.4cm) outer borders
    - Cut two 29" x 4 ½" (74 x 11.4cm) strips
    - Cut two 43" x 4 ½" (109 x 11.4cm) strips
- Pre-made binding or Half-yard of cotton solid cut into 2 ¼" (5.7cm) strips for binding totaling approximately 170" (432cm)
- One rectangle of cotton print 37" x 44" (94 x 112cm) for backing
- One rectangle of cotton batting at least 37" x 44" (94 x 112cm)
- Perle Cotton No. 12 in White (DMC 116/2-Blanc)

Note

This is a charm-pack friendly quilt, since each block is 5" (12.7cm). You could easily make it with a charm-pack of assorted solids if you don't have many in your stash.

INSTRUCTIONS

1 To assemble 20 blocks:
Sew each block in the following arrangement: the narrow solid strip is in the middle, with the large solid block on the left and the printed cotton on the right. Make 20 blocks and lay them out in five rows of four blocks. Reposition the blocks until you find a pleasing arrangement that balances the colors in your quilt.

2 Add white sashing between each block:
For each row, sew a 5" x 2 ½" (12.7 x 6.4cm) white strip between quilt blocks. So, you'll be adding three white strips per row. Please note the placement of each block in picture.

3 Add white sashing between each row, also at top and bottom:
Sew a 25" x 2 ½" (64 x 6.4cm) sash between all rows of blocks. Sew a sash to the top of all the rows, and also at the bottom.

4 Add white sashing to the sides of rows:
Sew a 35" x 2 ½" (89 x 6.4cm) white strip to the sides of the sewn rows.

5 Add borders:
Sew a 29" x 4 ½" (74 x 11.4cm) border to the top and bottom of quilt top. Sew a 43" x 4 ½" (109 x 11.4cm) border to each side of the quilt top. The quilt top is now complete.

6 Make the quilt sandwich:
Layer the quilt backing on the bottom, wrong side up. Cotton batting on top of this, and the quilt top (right side up) on top of the batting. Spray-baste all layers together or pin well.

7 Quilt by hand or by machine. I quilted mine by hand, using Perle cotton.

8 Bind the quilt:
Use pre-made double fold binding or, make your own binding by attaching 2 ¼" (5.7cm) strips of your chosen cotton solid until you have at least 170" (432cm) of binding. Press this strip in half, lengthwise. Bind using your preferred method. I machine sew my binding to the front of the quilt and sew it to the back by hand.

Back Side

Ruffle Collar Bib

ruffle collar bib

I do love a ruffle! Don't you? The fun part about this bib is that you could make it look sweet or you could make it look modern ~ either way, it's a simple and fast make with just the right amount of sweet. Need to make a bib for a baby boy? Skip the ruffle and attach the binding without it. The classic shape of this bib is perfect either way.

Finished Size
8" x 8" with 15" ties
20 x 20 cm with 38 cm ties

You will Need

- Two squares of cotton print fabric 8 ½" x 8 ½" (22 x 22cm) for bib front and back
- One strip of cotton print fabric 18" x 2 ¼" (46 x 5.7cm) for ruffle
- Binding cut on the bias 38" (97cm) in length
- One square of cotton batting 8 ¼" x 8 ¼" (21x 21 cm)
- Bib template
- Cardstock, cereal box or other cardboard for making the pattern

- Patch (linen + interfacing rectangles 2 ½" x 1 ¾") (6.4 x 4.4cm)
- Black thread
- Brown embroidery floss (DMC 3031)

INSTRUCTIONS

1 Trace the bib pattern to the wrong side of one square of bib fabric. Use the same pattern to cut a piece of cotton batting and spray-baste the cotton batting to wrong side of bib fabric, within the traced line. Lay the second bib fabric beneath this, with right sides facing, and sew along the traced line, leaving the neckline open.

2 Turn bib piece right side out and top stitch about a millimeter from edge. Quilt by machine or hand, as you like.

3 To make the ruffle, fold the ruffle strip's two short edges and one long edge towards the wrong side of fabric ¼" (.6cm) and press. Fold again, another ¼" (.6cm) and press. Stitch along all three sides to secure.

4 Next, set your sewing machine to its longest stitch length and sew along the long raw edge of ruffle strip. Remove this from the sewing machine leaving thread tails on each end. Knot the tails on one end. Pulling gently on one of the thread tails from the other side you'll notice the fabric beginning to gather. Fiddle with it, working the gathers down, and pulling on the thread to make more gathers. Do this until your ruffle measures 6 ½" (16.5cm). Center and pin the ruffle to the bib neckline,

attaching it with a zig-zag stitch. The ruffle will extend over each end of the bib neckline by about a ¼" (.6cm) per side. Trim off the ruffle's thread tails.

5 Center the bias cut binding strip at the center of bib. Using a fabric glue stick or pins, secure the binding over the ruffled neckline. Fold the raw edges at both ends of the binding inward and secure with glue stick or pins. Topstitch the binding from one end to the other. Tie a knot at both ends of the binding for

a finished look.

6 To make the patch, see the instructions at "My Favorite Patch." Embroider a running stitch border with three strands of brown floss. Use two strands of black thread to embroider the apple and strawberry design. Applique the patch by hand to the lower center of bib.

bear pillow

It's a bear. It's a pillow. It's the perfect combination of the two cuddliest things in the world ~ and every detail about this quilted pillow was chosen to keep it soft and snuggly. It has floppy ears a puffy smiling snout and appliqued fabric "buttons". I was inspired to make this pillow by my very own teddy bear ~ it sits atop a shelf in my sewing corner today. It's a little worn and dusty, but still looking good considering how much it was loved. As a child, I kissed this bear so much that his mouth wore off completely. And I hope someone somewhere does that to this bear, too.

Finished Size
16 ½" x 16 ½"
42 x 42 cm

YOU WILL NEED

- Ten squares of assorted cotton prints 4 ½" (11.4cm) for bear patchwork
- One square of an off-white or neutral print 5" (12.7cm) for the Half Square Triangles behind the bear's ears
- Two squares of cotton prints 5" (12.7cm) for HST's (you need two different prints for below each ear)
- One rectangle of blue cotton 16 ½" x 4 ½" (42 x 11.4cm) for pillow bottom
- Crochet trim 16 ½" in length (42cm)
- One square of cotton print 16 ½" (42cm) for back of pillow-front
- Two rectangles of cotton print 16 ½" x 12" (42 x 30.5cm) for pillow backing
- Two rectangles of linen 5" x 4" (12.7 x 10.2cm) for ears
- Two rectangles of brown cotton print 5" x 4" (12.7 x 10.2cm) for backs of ears
- One rectangle of linen 7" x 5" (17.8 x 12.7cm) for snout
- One rectangle of lightweight interfacing 7" x 5" (17.8 x 12.7cm) for snout
- One scrap of cotton print for buttons
- One scrap of cotton print for bear eyes
- One scrap of cotton print for bear nose
- Bear Pillow templates
- Cardstock, cereal box, or cardboard for patterns
- Fusible web
- One square of cotton batting 17" (43.2cm)
- Pre-made double fold binding or approximately 75" of 2 ¼" (191 x 5.7cm) strips of cotton for binding
- Brown embroidery floss (DMC 3031)
- Perle Cotton No.12 in Ecru (DMC 116/12-Ecru)
- Brown or black thread
- Polyfill stuffing

INSTRUCTIONS

1 Copy the bear templates and trace onto cardstock or thin cardboard to make patterns.

2 Trace the bear ear pattern onto the wrong side of two brown cotton prints for back of ears. Lay each on top of a linen rectangle and sew along traced line. Cut out the ear pieces, leaving a ¼" (.6cm) seam allowance and turn ears right side out. Embroider a running stitch ¾" (1.9cm)from the ear's edge with six strands of brown floss.

3 Cut the three 5" (12.7cm) squares diagonally to create half square triangles. With right sides facing, sew one colored half square triangle along its long edge to a neutral HST with the ear placed between them (centered). Watching the direction of the angle, repeat to sew an ear patch for opposite side. Press both ear blocks open so that the ear is laying flat against the neutral side of block and topstitch seam.

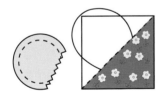

4 Arrange and sew together the patchwork:
-First row: ear block, two blocks, ear block
-Second row: 4 blocks
-Third row: 4 blocks

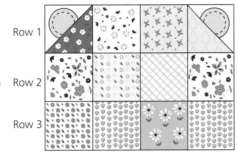

Row 1
Row 2
Row 3

5 Machine-baste the crochet trim to long edge of blue fabric, raw edges aligned.

6 Sew the bottom of the bear patchwork to the crochet trimmed edge of blue fabric, right sides facing. Press seam towards patchwork.

7 Make a quilt sandwich. Lay the 16 ½" (41.9cm) square of backing for pillow-front on the table, wrong side up. Lay the cotton batting on top of this. Lay the pillow-top on top of this, right side up. Spray-baste the layers together or pin well. Quilt by hand or machine. I quilted it by hand using Perle cotton No. 12 in

ecru (x's on the patchwork and straight lines across the pillow bottom).

8 Using the button template, cut two buttons from fusible web backed fabric. Press into place and machine applique to secure. Using the same colored thread, embroider an x to the center of each button.

9 Using the bear's eye template, cut two eyes from fusible web backed fabric. Press into place and machine applique to secure.

10 Create bear's snout by tracing the snout pattern onto the lightweight interfacing. Place interfacing on top of linen and sew along traced line. Using a seam ripper carefully cut a slit in the middle of the interfacing. Turn right side out and press. Using the nose

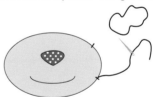

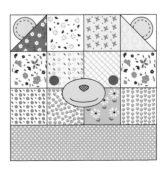

template, cut a nose from fusible web backed fabric. Press onto the linen snout piece. Machine applique to secure. Using six strands of brown floss, backstitch the bear's mouth. Applique the bear's snout by hand onto the patchwork (as pictured), and when there is a 2" (5cm) opening left, lightly stuff the snout with polyfill. Finish appliqueing the snout closed.

11 Make the back of pillow by folding a long edge of a 16 ½" x 12" (41.9 x 30.5cm) rectangle to the wrong side 1" (2.5cm). Fold again 1" (2.5cm) and sew the hem. Repeat for second rectangle of pillow back.

12 Fold and pin the bear's ears out of way, then lay the pillow-front right side down. Lay the pillow backing rectangles on top (right sides up) so that they overlap at the center. Pin in place and sew around all four edges.

13 Attach pre-made double fold binding or, make your own binding by sewing 2 ¼" (5.7cm) strips of your chosen cotton print until you have approximately 75" (191cm) of binding. Press this strip in half, lengthwise. Bind using your preferred method. I machine sew my binding to the front of the quilt and sew it to the back by hand.

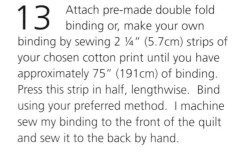

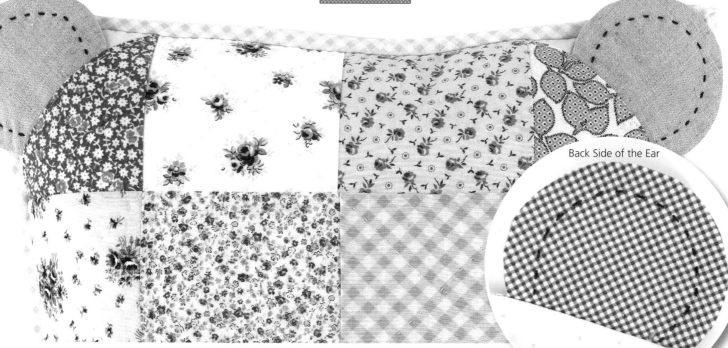

Back Side of the Ear

ABC tote bag

I had in mind the oversized picture books my children bring home from the library when I designed this tote. Those books are filled with big, bright illustrations and large print, so a library book bag has to be roomy enough to hold those big ideas. Inside this one, there's a pocket for reading lists well as a pocket on the front to hold a library card. Of course, this bag could just as easily carry a towel and a water bottle to the beach. Or, ballet shoes and leg warmers. Soccer cleats and shin guards. Whatever they'll need it for, this tote will come in handy!

Finished Size
15 ½" x 12 ½" x 3"
39.4 x 32 x 7.6 cm

YOU WILL NEED

- Two rectangles of red ticking canvas 19 ½" x 6" (49.5 x 15.2cm) for bag bottom
- Two rectangles of alphabet cotton print 19 ½" x 9" (49.5 x 23cm) for bag upper
- Two rectangles of Ultra-firm interfacing 19 ½" x 14 ½" (49.5 x 36.8cm)
- Two strips of blue pin dot print 19 ½" x 2 ¼" (49.5 x 5.7cm) for bag binding
- Two rectangles of cotton print 19 ½" x14 ¼" (49.5 x 36.2cm) for bag lining
- One rectangle of linen 4" x 5" (10.1 x 12.7cm) for front pocket
- One rectangle of solid white cotton 4" x 4 ½" (10.1 x 11.4cm) for front pocket backing
- One rectangle of red ticking canvas 8" x 6 ½" (20.3 x 16.5cm) for inner pocket
- One rectangle of red ticking canvas 8" x 8 ¾" (20.3 x 22.2cm) for inner pocket
- Single fold binding 30" (76.2cm) for inner pocket binding
- Two cotton-webbing handles 18" (45.7cm) in length, 36" (91.4cm) total
- 4 squares of linen 2 ¼" (5.7cm) for handle patches
- 4 squares of lightweight interfacing 2 ¼" (5.7cm) for handle patches
- "Abc" embroidery design
- One ribbon 2" (5.1 cm) in length
- Brown embroidery floss (DMC 3031)
- One red button 1" (2.5cm)
- Two pearl snaps

INSTRUCTIONS

1 Sew one piece of red ticking canvas to alphabet print along the long edge, right sides facing. Press seam towards the ticking, fuse interfacing to wrong side and top stitch twice along the seam, sewing the lines a millimeter apart. Repeat for back of bag.

2 Press the two binding strips in half lengthwise. Align the raw edges to the top of alphabet cotton print and sew to attach. Press the binding up. Repeat for back of bag.

3 Make the pocket. Cut the 4" x 5" (10.1 x 12.7cm) rectangle of linen into two pieces ~ 1 ¼" x 4" (3.2 x 10.2cm) and 3 ¾" x 4" (9.5 x 10.2cm). Fold 2" (5.1cm) ribbon in half and center between the two linen pieces, raw edges aligned. Sew ¼" (.6cm) seam. Press towards the shorter piece of linen so that the ribbon is hanging down over the larger piece. Trace embroidery design onto lower portion of pocket. I embroidered the design using the backstitch and three strands of brown floss. With right sides

facing, sew the solid white backing piece to the pocket piece, leaving a 2" (5.1cm) opening along the side for turning right side out. Clip the corners. Turn right side out, easing out the corners, and press well. Sew on big red button above the ribbon. Embroider a running stitch border along the lower portion of pocket. Sew pocket to front of bag, centered and 2" (5.1cm) above the ticking stripes.

4 With right sides facing, pin bag front and back together. Sew along sides and bottom of bag. Fold bottom corners into a triangle and mark a 3"

(7.6cm) line. Stitch across this line; repeat on other side.

10.1x12.7 cm - 3 ¾"

1½" (3,8 cm)   1½" (3,8 cm)

3" (7,6 cm)

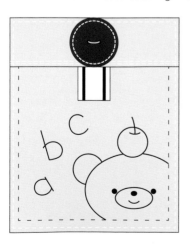

5 Sew bag lining. Pin the two lining pieces together, right sides facing and sew along the sides and bottom. Fold the bottom corners into triangles and mark a 3" (7.6cm) line. Stitch across this line; repeat on other side. Place the lining inside the bag (wrong sides facing) and pin well across the top. Starting 1" (2.5cm) from each side seam, machine-baste into place along the raw edge of the lining.

6 Make the inside pocket. (If you don't have single fold binding, make some of your own. Cut a strip of fabric 30" x 1 ¼" (76.2 x 3.2cm), and press in half lengthwise. Next, fold the raw edges in towards the center crease and press.) Attach 8" (20.3cm) of binding across the red ticking piece 8" x 6 ½" (20.3 x 16.5cm). With wrong sides both facing up, pin the 8" x 8 ¾" (20.3 x 22.2cm)

piece of red ticking to the 8" x 6 ½" (20.3 x 16.5cm) pocket piece, aligned at the bottom. Fold the shorter piece over to the front, so right sides are facing up, and press so the seam is now inside. Sew a 3/8" (1cm) seam along the bottom edge to enclose the raw seam. Attach binding to both sides of pocket, folding in the raw edges of binding at bottom of sides. Top of the pocket will have all raw edges. Pin the binding at the top of bag out of the way and machine-baste the pocket along its raw edge, inside of bag, centered on the bag's raw edge.

7 Press binding at the top of the bag over the raw edges, to lining. Pin or glue stick in place. Sew by hand or machine.

8 Machine-sew handles to bag, 5" (12.7cm) apart from center and 1"

(2.5cm) below the binding. Repeat for both sides of bag.

9 Sew four linen squares to the light-weight interfacing, around all four edges. Using a seam ripper, cut a slit in the middle of the interfacing and turn patches right side out. Ease out corners and press well. Embroider a running stitch border around the four patches. Applique the patches by hand over the raw edges of handles.

10 Optionally, add pearl snaps to the sides of the bag. Follow manufacturer's instructions and place each snap 1 ¼" (3.2cm) down from top edge and 1 ¼" (3.2cm) out from the side seam.

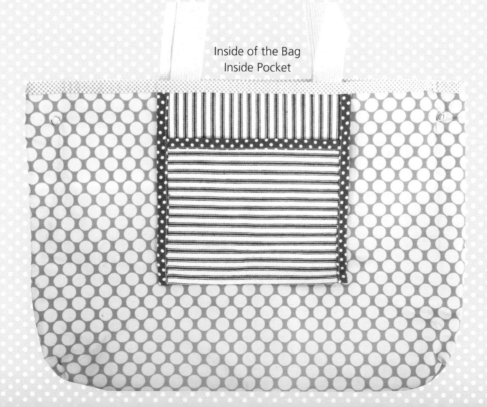

Inside of the Bag
Inside Pocket

"mouse house doll quilt"

This is a doll quilt that your little one will love playing with due to its peek-a-boo "mouse house" flaps. I've put cute little mice inside my houses but I think a different animal behind each flap would be a lot of fun, too. Even better if you could find sleeping animals to match perfectly with this mini-quilt's embroidered messages: "Sweet dreams, Sleep tight, I love you, Good night!"

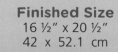

Finished Size
16 ½" x 20 ½"
42 x 52.1 cm

Sweet dreams

Sleep tight

I love you

Goodnight!

YOU WILL NEED

- Forty-one squares of assorted cotton prints 2 ½" (6.4cm) for patchwork
- Four squares of novelty mouse prints 2 ½" (6.4cm) for under the house flaps
- Two squares of text print 3 ¼" (8.3cm) (cut into HST's) for house roof background
- Two squares of text print 2 ½" (6.4cm) (cut into HST's) for house roof background
- Two squares of brown dot print 2 ½" (6.4cm) (cut into HST's) for house roof
- Four strips of pale pink cotton solid 17" x 2 ½" (43.2 x 6.4cm) for sashes
- Four squares of cotton print 2 ½" (6.4cm) for "house" flaps (front)
- Four squares of text print 2 ½" (6.4cm) for "house" flaps (back)
- Four rectangles of white cotton solid 1 ¼" x 1 ¾" (3.2 x 4.4cm) for doors
- One rectangle of cotton print 17" x 21" (43.2 x 53.3cm) for quilt backing
- One rectangle of cotton batting 17" x 21" (43.2 x 53.3cm)
- Double-fold binding or at least 88" of 2 ¼" (224 x 5.7cm) strips of cotton print to make your own binding
- Four small buttons
- Brown embroidery floss (DMC 3860)
- Coral embroidery floss (DMC 3705)
- Silver Metallic embroidery floss (DMC E168)
- Perle Cotton No. 12 in white
- Quilting ruler (that shows 45 degree)

INSTRUCTIONS

1 Cut the two 2 ½" (6.4cm) text print squares diagonally to result in four half square triangles (HST's). Cut the two brown dot print squares into HST's. Pair these triangles together (text on one side, brown dot on the other), right sides facing, and sew along one short side. Press the seam towards the brown dot fabric. Trim these four pieced triangles with a quilting ruler so that they each measure half of a 2 ¾" (7cm) square.

2 Cut the two (8.3cm) text print squares into HST's and pair these with the triangles you've just pieced, right sides facing, and sew along the long side. Press the seam towards the pieced triangles. Trim each block to a perfect 2 ½" (6.4cm) square, lining up the diagonal seam with the 45 degree angle on your quilting ruler. You have completed the four "roof" blocks.

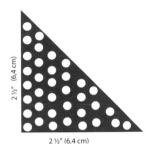

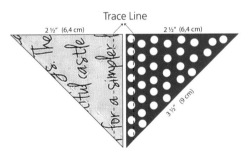

Trace Line

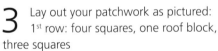

3 Lay out your patchwork as pictured:
1st row: four squares, one roof block, three squares
2nd row: four squares, one mouse print, three squares
3rd row: one square, one roof block, four squares, one roof block, one square
4th row: one square, one mouse print, four squares, one mouse print, one square
5th row: three squares, one roof block, four squares
6th row: three squares, one mouse print, four squares
Sew each row together, pressing all seams to one side, switching directions for each row.

4 Sew row 1 to row 2. Sew row 3 to row 4. Sew row 5 to row 6. Press all seams up, in the direction of the roof blocks. You have completed the patchwork.

5 Sew one light pink sashing strip (17" x 2 ½") (43.2 x 6.4cm) before and after each group of patchwork, as pictured. Press all seams in the direction of the sashing.

6 Trace the embroidery designs onto quilt, as pictured.
-The moon and stars and "Sweet dreams" is located 2" (5.1cm) in from the right side, ½" (1.3cm) above the patchwork.
-"Sleep tight" is located 2" (5.1cm) in from the left side, ½" (1.3cm) below the patchwork.
-"I love you" is located 2" (5.1cm) in from the right side, ½" (1.3cm) below the patchwork.
-"Goodnight!" is located 2" (5.1cm) in from the left side, ½" (1.3cm) below the patchwork.
Embroider all the words with three strands of coral floss in backstitch. Embroider the moon and stars with two strands of silver floss in backstitch.

7 Make the quilt sandwich. Lay out quilt backing piece on table (wrong side up) and smooth. Lay cotton batting on top. Lay quilt top (right side up) on top of batting. Spray-baste together or pin well. Quilt as desired. I hand-quilted mine using silver floss on the sashing, white perle cotton on the patchwork, and three strands of brown floss to embroider a running stitch along the sides and bottom of the mouse print blocks.

8 Bind the quilt:
Use pre-made double fold binding or, make your own binding by attaching 2 ¼" (5.7cm) strips of your chosen cotton print until you have at least 88" (224cm) of binding. Press this strip in half, lengthwise. Bind using your preferred method.

I machine sew my binding to the front of the quilt and sew it to the back by hand.

9 To make the house flaps, sew the front pieces to the backs, right sides facing, leaving a 1 ¾" (4.4cm) opening at the top (the side you will be attaching to the quilt). Clip the corners. Turn the house flaps right side out, easing out the corners, and press well.

10 To make the doors, lay out your solid white rectangles, right sides

facing down on your ironing board. Use your glue stick to aid in pressing back a ¼" (0.6cm) edge on each side of the four rectangles. Sew by hand or machine onto the house flaps. Using two strands of the brown floss, embroider a running stitch around the sides and top of each door. Sew a button on each door.

11 Pin each house flap onto the quilt, just below a roof block, and topstitch in place (backstitch at the beginning and end).

crayon castle caddy

Keeping the kids' crayons neat and tidy in fussy organizers never seems to work at my house. If the crayons have to be placed in individual slots and there's only enough room for one pack of crayons, it's not going to work. Letting them throw all their crayons into a cup a few handfuls at a time ~ yes, please! A cup with an attached lid... and it's all as cute as can be? Yes, yes, yes!!! I daresay it's the best crayon caddy ever.

Finished Size
3 ¼" x 6"
8.3 x 15.2 cm

YOU WILL NEED

- One rectangle of cotton print 4 ¼" x 10 ¾" (10.8 x 27.3cm) for cup exterior
- One rectangle of cotton print 4 ¼" x 10 ¾" (10.8 x 27.3cm) for cup lining
- One rectangle of cotton print 7" x 5 ½" (17.8 x 14cm) for lid exterior
- One rectangle of cotton print 7" x 5 ½" (17.8 x 14cm) for lid lining
- One strip of binding cut on the bias 12" x 1 ¼" (30.5 x 3.2cm) for lid binding
- One square of linen 5" (12.7cm) for bottom of cup
- One rectangle of cotton batting 10 ¼" x 3 ½" (26 x 8.9cm)
- One rectangle of ultra-firm stabilizer 10 ¼" x 3 ½" (26 x 8.9cm)
- One square of ultra-firm stabilizer 3 ¼" (8.3cm)
- Crayon Castle Caddy templates
- Cardstock, cereal box, or other thin cardboard for making patterns and cup insert
- One piece of ribbon 2" (5.1cm) in length
- ½" - ¾" (1.3 – 1.9cm) wool felt ball

- Patch (linen + interfacing rectangles 3 ½" x 1 ¾") (8.9 x 4.4cm)
- Brown embroidery floss (DMC 3031)
- "c" – Teal embroidery floss (DMC 959)
- "r" - Orange embroidery floss (DMC 922)
- "a" - Pink embroidery floss (DMC 894)
- "y" - Red embroidery floss (DMC 349)
- "o" - Blue embroidery floss (DMC 3810)
- "n" - Purple embroidery floss (DMC 209)
- "s" - Green embroidery floss (DMC 563)

INSTRUCTIONS

1 Use the templates to make your patterns with the cardstock or thin cardboard. From the ultra firm stabilizer cut a rectangle 10 ¼" x 3 ½" (26 x 8.9cm), a circle, and a lid piece. Use the circle pattern to cut one extra cardboard circle (this will go inside the cup, to act as a bottom, and can always be replaced with new cardboard as it gets dirty.)

2 Glue-stick the lid stabilizer piece to the wrong side of lid lining fabric. Sew along the curved edge ¼" (.6cm) to secure. Cut the lid lining fabric directly along the curved edge of the stabilizer, but cut an extra ¼" (.6cm) seam allowance along the straight edges. Fold this piece, right sides facing, so that the straight edges are aligned. Sew directly along the straight edge of the stabilizer, backstitching at both ends. Snip the point and press the seam open. Now you have a lined cone shape.

3 Trace lid pattern to the wrong side of lid exterior fabric. Cut an extra ¼" (.6cm) seam allowance along the straight lines. Fold fabric in half, right sides facing and sew along the straight edge, backstitching at both ends. Snip point and press seam open. Turn right side out. Slide the exterior cone onto lining cone, aligning the seams. Pin the layers together, making sure the layers are smooth and snug. Sew a 1/8" (.3cm) seam around bottom edge to secure. Machine-baste the 2" (5.1cm) piece of ribbon at the center of the exterior lid seam, right sides facing, aligned at the raw edge.

4 Attach pre-made single fold bias binding to raw edge of lid, or cut a strip of fabric 12" x 1 ¼" (30.5 x 3.2cm) on the bias to make your own. Attach bias binding. (You may do this by machine or hand. I sewed the binding by machine to the front. I had pre-pressed a ¼" (.6cm) fold along the other long side. Folding this to the back, I used a glue stick and iron to hold it in place. Then I stitched it by hand.

5 Make the cup. Lay lining rectangle, wrong side up. Layer batting first,

then stabilizer on top of the lining, ¼" (.6cm) down from top edge, 1/2" (1.3cm) up from bottom edge, and centered on the sides (1/4" (.6cm) in from either side). Mark horizontal lines across the stabilizer 1" (2.5cm) from the top and bottom. Starting and ending at the raw edges of fabric, sew across the marked lines. Mark vertical lines ¼" (.6cm) in from the stabilizer's short edge. Starting and ending at the raw edges, sew along the marked lines.

6 Turn piece over so right side of lining is facing up. Align the raw edge

of the ribbon (attached to lid) to the top of lining, ¼" (.6cm) in from one side. Machine-baste in place. Make sure the lining of the lid is facing the right side of cup lining for proper placement. Carefully fold the lid flat and pin to keep it out of the way during the rest of the sewing process.

7 Pin the exterior fabric, right sides facing, to the lining piece and sew a ¼" (.6cm) seam across the top edge (where batting and stabilizer are located ¼" (.6cm) from top). Press the seam open and fold the piece in half so that the short ends of the exterior are facing and the short ends of the lining are facing. Sew a ¼" (.6cm) seam along this end. Now pull the exterior fabric down over the stabilizer so its right side is facing out and the lining is facing inside. Pull on the

fabric until the top edge is smooth and there is a ½" (1.3cm) of raw fabric at the bottom.

8 Make the bottom of cup. Glue-stick the stabilizer circle onto the wrong side of bottom linen fabric. Cut the linen around the stabilizer with an extra ¾" (2cm) seam allowance. No need to be exact here. Make a running stitch around edge of fabric using a stitch length of about ¼" (.6cm). Pull the thread tails tightly around circle and knot. Press and machine stitch a ¼" (.6cm) around circle edge to secure.

9 Fingerpress the bottom edge of exterior fabric to inside. Pin if you like. Sew the bottom linen circle to the bottom exterior edge using short invisible whipstitches, making sure the neat side of

linen circle is facing out and the raw side is inside the cup. Smooth down the raw ends of fabric inside the cup and push the cardboard circle to the bottom, to cover them up. It will fit very snuggly and will not move out of place.

10 Sew wool felt ball to pointy part of lid. Hide thread tails in between the layers of the lid.

11 To make the patch, see the instructions at "My Favorite Patch". Embroider a running stitch border with three strands of brown floss. Use three strands of each designated floss color to embroider the word "crayons". Applique the patch by hand to the center of the crayon cup.

on the spot trivet

I love putting my hot bowls and dishes on handmade trivets ~ they add even more beauty to the table. This trivet showcases 15 of your favorite fabrics and puts them on the spot! Use a mix of prints ~ like dots, novelties, ginghams, small florals and text prints~ for a fun look. Set against the natural linen, every spot will stand out!

Finished Size
10" x 10"
25.4 x 25.4 cm

YOU WILL NEED

- Two squares of linen 10" (25.4cm) for base front and back
- Fifteen assorted fabric prints 2 ½" (6.4cm) squares for circle appliques
- Lightweight interfacing (NON-fusible)
- One square of cotton batting 9 ½" (24.1cm)
- One square of Insul-Bright batting 9 ½" (24.1cm)
- One piece of Crochet trim 41" (104cm) in length
- Circle template 2 ½" (6.4cm)
- Cardstock, Cereal box or other cardboard to make a template
- Perle Cotton No. 8 in Ecru (DMC 116/8-Ecru)
- Brown embroidery floss (DMC 839)
- Seam ripper

- Patch (linen + interfacing squares 2 ¼") (5.7cm)
- Template "Bon Café"
- Black thread
- Brown embroidery floss (DMC 839)
- Peach embroidery floss (DMC 967)
- Pale pink embroidery floss (DMC 151)
- Green embroidery floss (DMC 988)

INSTRUCTIONS

1 Spray-baste the cotton batting to center of a linen square. Next spray-baste the Insul-Bright batting on top of the cotton batting. Using perle cotton no. 8 in ecru, baste several stitches through these three layers to hold everything securely in place when turning right side out.

2 On the second square of linen, machine baste crochet trim around all four sides of the front, raw edges aligned.

3 Place the two squares of linen together, right sides facing. Sew a ¼" (.6cm) seam around all four sides, leaving a 3" (7.6cm) opening for turning right side out. Turn right side out, ease out the corners, and press well. Handstitch the opening closed.

4 To make the circle patches, use the 2 ½" (6.4cm) circle template to create a cardboard pattern. Trace fifteen circles onto the wrong side of assorted fabric prints. Lay them right side down, traced side up, onto a square of lightweight interfacing. Sew around the traced line, overlapping stitches. Cut with scissors (I used pinking shears) around the sewn line, leaving slightly less than a ¼" (0.6cm) seam allowance. Using a seam ripper, carefully cut a small opening at the center of the interfacing. Turn right side out through this opening, and press well. Repeat until all fifteen circle patches are prepared.

5 Applique the circle patches onto the linen trivet in rows of four, as pictured, leaving the last spot open for the patch.

6 To make the patch, see the instructions at "My Favorite Patch." Embroider a running stitch border with three strands of brown floss. Use two strands of black thread to embroider the words "Bon Café" and also to outline the peach. Use two strands of peach floss to fill one side of the peach. Use two strands of the pale pink floss to fill the other side of the peach. Use two strands of the green floss to fill the leaf. Applique the patch by hand to the lower right side corner of the trivet.

7 Use three strands of brown floss to embroider a running stitch around all the circle patches.

stacked hexagon mug rug

One day I was playing with hexagons and
realized a stacked hexagon
flower in graduated sizes made the perfect landing spot for my teacup! A cup of
tea is always by my side while I'm working. Some days there's a cookie too, but
other days I'm on a diet. One thing is sure,
though, I like my teacup safe and cozy.
And just in case you're not on a diet, I've
designed this mug rug with a useful pocket. There's just enough room for a tea bag
and one giant cookie.
Enjoy!

Finished Size
8" x 9 ¼"
20.3 x 23.5 cm

YOU WILL NEED

- Two rectangles of linen 8 ½" x 9 ¾" (21.6 x 24.8cm) for base front and back
- One rectangle of linen 8 ½" x 2 ¼" (21.6 x 5.6cm) for pocket
- One strip of green print 8 ½" x 1 1/8" (21.6 x 2.9cm) for pocket binding
- Assorted fabric scraps for Hexagon flowers
- Green fabric scraps for leaves
- One rectangle of cotton batting 8 ½" x 9 ¼" (21.6 x 23.5cm)
- Paper Hexagon templates
- Leaf template
- Paper
- One ribbon 1 ½" (3.8cm) in length
- Green embroidery floss (DMC 701)
- Green thread
- Fusible web

- Patch (linen + interfacing rectangles 2 ¼" x 1 ¾") (5.7 x 4.4cm)
- Black thread
- Brown embroidery floss (DMC 3031)

INSTRUCTIONS

1 To make the stacked hexagon flower, start by cutting your templates. From each of the three hexagon templates (1 ¼" hexagon, 1" hexagon, ½" hexagon) (3.2cm hexagon, 2.5cm hexagon, 1.3cm hexagon), cut seven hexagon pattern papers. Using the hexagon pattern papers as a guide, cut your fabric hexagons ~ each approximately 3/8" (1cm) larger on all sides than the paper pattern.

2 To make the hexagon patches, pin or use a light spray of adhesive to position the paper pattern to the center of the wrong side of fabric. Next, fold back an edge of fabric to the paper side, and finger pressing along the way, use a needle and thread to make basting stitches right through fabric and paper. Baste around all edges, in the same way. Continue until all of the hexagon patches are basted.

3 To make a hexagon flower, sew all seven equally sized hexagon patches together in the form of a rosette. Begin by placing two hexagons together, right sides facing, and with a knotted thread, whipstitch along an edge, keeping your stitches uniform and neat. When you get to the end of a side, backstitch a few times and then continue, adding hexagons until you've sewn a rosette. When finished, press well, spray with starch if you like. Carefully remove your basting stitches and pattern papers now. (The papers can be used again.)

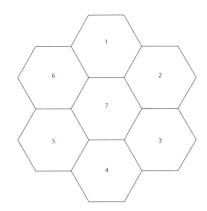

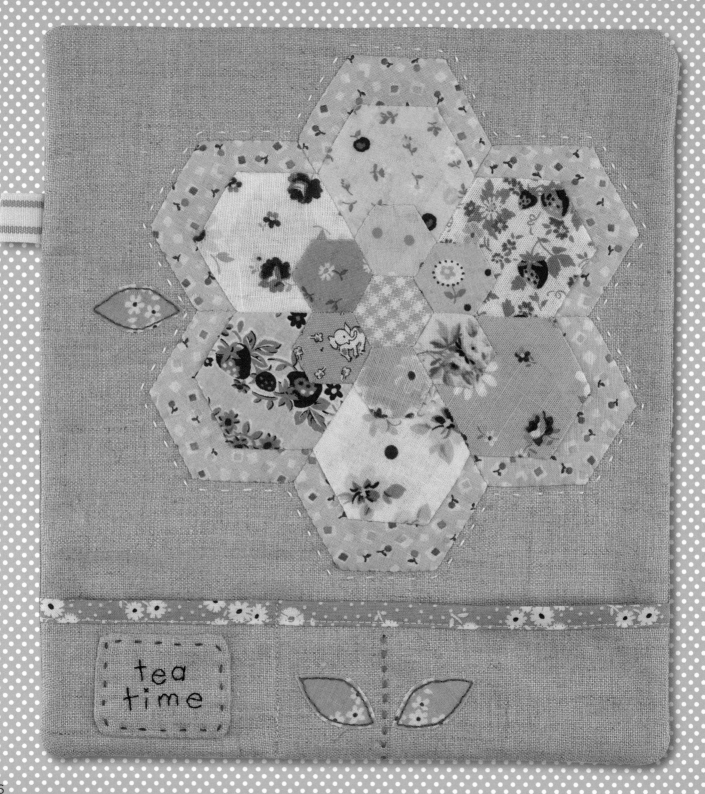

tea
time

4 Hand-applique the smallest hexagon rosette to the center of the medium hexagon rosette, carefully aligned so that the side seams match, as pictured. Center the medium sized rosette atop the large rosette and line it up carefully so the side seams match in a straight line. Lastly, stitch the large hexagon rosette onto the linen front piece, ¾" (1.9cm) in from the upper right hand corner.

5 Position the linen pocket piece atop the linen front to find the center of the hexagon flower to mark a line for the stem. Use six strands of green floss to embroider a running stitch "stem".

6 Use the leaf template to cut three leaves from green fabric scraps that have been backed with fusible web. Press two leaves on either side of the stem, centered. Position the last leaf at the center of the hexagon flower on the left side. Machine applique the leaves into place using green thread.

7 Press the pocket binding strip in half lengthwise. Press raw edges in towards center fold. Sew binding to top of linen pocket piece.

8 Pin the linen pocket piece atop of linen front, aligned at bottom edge.

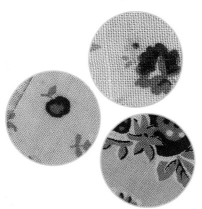

Machine-baste in place 1/8" (0.3cm) from raw edge.

9 Fold the 1 ½" (3.8cm) length of ribbon in half and align raw edges to the left side of linen front piece, 2 ½" (6.4cm) down from the top. Machine-baste in place.

10 Lay the linen front and back pieces right sides together, and place on top of cotton batting. Pin and sew around all four edges leaving a 2" (5.1cm) opening for turning. Turn right side out, ease out all corners, and press well. Slipstitch the opening closed.

11 To divide the pocket, mark a line 3" (7.6cm) from the left hand side. Machine stitch along this line, backstitching at beginning and end.

12 To make the patch, see the instructions at "My Favorite Patch". Embroider a running stitch border with three strands of brown floss. Use two strands of black thread to embroider the words "tea time." Applique the patch by hand to the center of left side pocket.

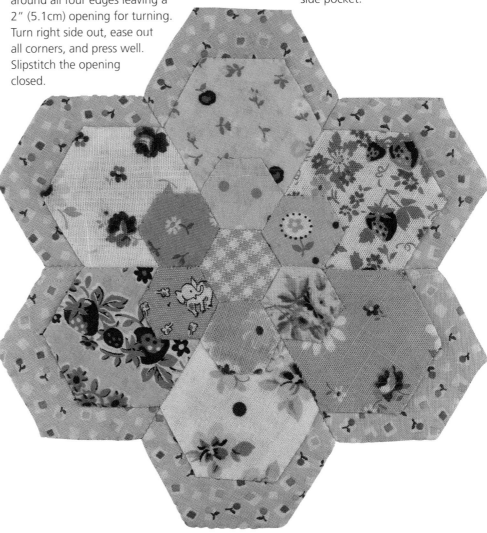

ric-rac coasters

Your friends will be envious. And nothing could be simpler to make than these ric-rac trimmed coasters that aren't just pretty ~ their real job is to protect your table. They can't help being so charming. Sewing them can be quite addictive as it's fun to play with all sorts of prints and colors. Here, I've made a set using a single floral print, putting the focus on the ric-rac, but I also like making sets with mismatched prints. When gifting a set of coasters for one of those envious friends, tie them with ribbon for a cute presentation. Include some fancy stripey straws and a bottle of sparkling berry lemonade ~ perfection!

Finished Size
4 ¼" x 4 ¼"
10.8 x 10.8 cm

ALL NATURAL
WITH PURE
CANE SUGAR
BRAND
LEMON
TRADE MARK
to: Mia

YOU WILL NEED

• Eight squares of cotton fabric 4 ½" (11.4cm) for coaster exterior

• Four squares of medium weight fusible interfacing 4" (10.1cm)

• Four pieces of ric-rac in various colors 18 ½" (47cm) in length each (74" total) (188cm)

• Four pieces of cotton ribbon 1 ¾" (4.4cm) in length each (7" total) (17.8cm)

INSTRUCTIONS

1 Lay out four cotton squares of exterior fabric on your ironing board, right side facing down. Position a piece of fusible interfacing onto the center of each square. Make sure to lay the fusible side of interfacing to wrong side of exterior fabric. Press with a hot iron to fuse together.

2 Sew ric-rac onto the fabric squares backed with interfacing. Make sure to sew ric-rac to the right side of fabric. Use a ¼" (.6cm) seam and note that the ric-rac on the inside of the stitch line is what you will see when the coasters are finished. (Ric-rac on the outside of the stitch line, on the side of the raw edge, will be hidden inside the coaster.) Ease the ric-rac around the corners. When you come around to the point where the ric-rac began, curve the ric-rac down towards the raw edge, finish sewing and trim off any extra ric-rac. See pic. Repeat until you've sewn ric-rac around all four squares.

3 Fold one length of ribbon in half so that it is now 7/8" (2.2cm) long. Align the raw edges of ribbon to a raw edge of the square, right sides facing. Machine-baste in place. Repeat for all four squares.

4 Lay the remaining four exterior fabric squares on top of the ric-rac and ribbon trimmed squares (right sides facing) and pin together. For each, sew a ¼" (.6cm) seam around all four edges, leaving a 2" (5cm) opening at the center of a side for turning right side out.

5 Turn coaster right side out through opening, ease out the corners, and press well. Topstitch 1/8" (.3cm) from edge. Repeat until all four coasters are completed.

ns

thread

small things fabric boxes

These fabric boxes are my fave. Sweet, charming, unfussy... They make great little organizers inside your drawers, but they're also pretty enough to display anywhere throughout the house. I'd love to see a whole row of them in my sewing room someday. I could picture a red fabric box for my red buttons, an orange box for my orange buttons, and so on and so on... you get the picture.

Finished Size
3" x 3" x 3"
7.6 x 7.6 x 7.6 cm

TO MAKE ONE BOX
YOU WILL NEED

• Five squares of cotton print 3 ½" (8.9cm) for exterior fabric (box sides and top of lid)

• One rectangle of cotton print 3 ½" x 1 ½" (8.9 x 3.8cm) for contrasting lid flap

• One rectangle of cotton print 3 ½" x 5" (8.9 x 12.7cm) for lid lining

• Six squares of cotton print 3 ½" (8.9cm) for bottom of box and lining

• Six squares of mid-weight fusible interfacing 3" (7.6cm)

• One rectangle of mid-weight fusible interfacing 1 ¼" x 3" (3.2 x 7.6cm) for lid flap

• One piece of ½" (1.3cm) wide ric-rac 12" (30cm) in length

• Lid flap templates

• Cardstock or thin board to make patterns

• Button

• Patch (linen + interfacing rectangles 2 ¼" x 1 ¾") (5.7 x 4.4cm)

• Brown embroidery floss (DMC 3031)

• Light blue embroidery floss (DMC 3811)

• Light pink embroidery floss (DMC 224)

• Yellow embroidery floss (DMC 834)

INSTRUCTIONS

1 To make the lid, press one square of interfacing to the wrong side of one square of exterior fabric, centered. (To truly center the interfacing you may prefer to lightly draw ¼" (.6cm) lines along each edge of the fabric square. The interfacing should be placed precisely within these lines.) Using the lid flap pattern, cut a contrasting lid flap piece. Using the lid-interfacing pattern, cut one piece of interfacing. Fuse this to the center of the wrong side of contrasting lid flap piece. With right sides facing, sew the straight edge of the contrasting lid flap to one side of the square lid piece. Press the seam open. Attach the ric-rac to the right side of fabric in a long U-shape, as pictured. With right sides facing, sew the lid lining to the lid piece, in the same U-shape. Don't sew the straight edge opposite the curved end of lid. Turn lid right side out and press well. Set aside.

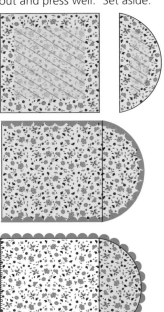

2 Press one square of interfacing to the center of the wrong side of the bottom fabric for box. (At this point accuracy becomes more important and I recommend lightly drawing those ¼" (.6cm) lines on all your fabric squares.) Press one square of interfacing to the wrong side of each of the four exterior fabric squares (these are the box's sides), centered.

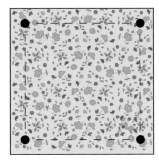

3 Sew the squares together as shown in the picture (from point to point, NOT sewing into the usual ¼" (.6cm) seam allowance) ~ backstitching at the beginning and end of each seam. Sew the four sides to the bottom of box, right sides facing, and press the seams towards the sides.

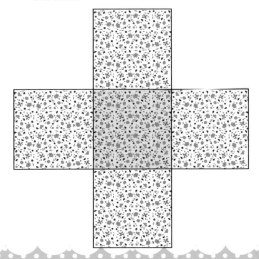

4 With right sides facing and raw edges aligned, sew the lid piece to the end of a side square, sewing from point to point. Make sure the lid does not extend into the ¼" (.6cm) seam allowance on either side of the interfacing.

5 Next, sew all of the sides together, right sides facing, starting from the raw edges and sewing down to the seam allowance, but not into it. (Backstitch once you reach the seam allowance.) Press all seams open. The exterior box is complete.

6 To sew the lining, draw ¼" (.6cm) lines on the wrong side of five lining squares. Sew the lining squares, just as you did the exterior (from point to point) but sew just outside the drawn lines so that the lining is slightly smaller and fits into the box more smoothly. When finished, press the raw top edge to the wrong side of fabric ¼" (.6cm).

7 Press the box exterior's raw edges to the inside ¼" (.6cm). Use a fabric glue stick to secure. Place the lining inside and sew around all four edges by hand using a blind stitch.

8 Sew a button to the lid flap.

9 To make a patch, see the instructions at "My Favorite Patch." Embroider a running stitch border with three strands of floss that matches the color of the ric-rac on that box. Embroider the words, "thread", "buttons", or "pins" using three strands of brown floss. Applique the patch by hand to the front of the fabric box, centered and approximately one centimeter from the bottom edge.

jam jar pin cushion

We go through a lot of jam in this house. Strawberry jam on toast with butter ~ yum! I save the empty jars for storing little things and I love the look so much, I've even made a pincushion in the shape of one! My favorite details are the super flat bottom and, of course, the red gingham cut on the bias. It would make a sweet gift for your friends who sew and you could even embroider their names on each "label".

Finished Size
2 ¾" x 3 ½"
7 x 8.9 cm

You will Need

- One rectangle of linen 9" x 3 ¼" (22.9 x 8.3cm) for base of jar
- One square of linen 5" (12.7cm) for jar bottom
- One strip of red gingham cut on the bias 9" x 2 ¼" (22.9 x 5.7cm) for jar lid binding
- One square of red gingham 6" (15.2cm) for jar lid
- One piece of crochet trim 9" (22.9cm) in length
- One rectangle of cotton batting 8 ½" x 9 ¼" (21.6 x 23.5cm)
- Jam Jar circle template
- Cereal box or other thin cardboard
- Perle Cotton No. 8 in black (DM 116/8-310)

- Patch (linen + interfacing rectangles 2 ½" x 1 ¾") (6.4 x 4.4cm)
- Pink wool felt scrap for strawberry
- Black embroidery floss (DMC 310)
- Green embroidery floss (DMC 988)

INSTRUCTIONS

1 Sew crochet trim to top of linenbase, raw edges aligned. Fold the strip of red gingham for lid binding in half lengthwise. Sew to the crochet trimmed edge of linen, raw edges aligned. Press binding up. Fold the linen rectangle in half so that the crochet trim and gingham binding face each other on the inside. Sew along the side edge (3 ¼" edge) (8.3cm) and then zig-zag stitch the edge. Turn right side out.

2 Hand-sew the red gingham binding to inside of jar.

3 Trace the jam jar circle template onto cereal box or equally sturdy cardboard. Enclosed in linen, this actual cardboard will be the base of your pincushion, allowing it to sit completely flat. Trace the cardboard circle onto the 5" (12.7cm) square of linen and cut a circle approximately 1" (2.5cm) larger. Folding in ¼" (.6cm) of fabric as you go around, sew stitches in the fold with a double length of thread. Stitches should be made a centimeter in length, around the full circle. Pull the thread tails tight and make a few extra stitches to secure, then tie a knot.

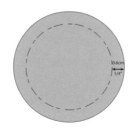

0.6cm
¼"

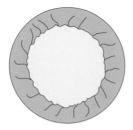

4 Finger press a ¼" (.6cm) fold of linen all around the bottom of the jar towards the inside. Pinching this fold, little by little, against the linen-enclosed cardboard circle, whipstitch all the way around, making sure the neat side of the

linen circle is facing outwards. Overlap stitches when you get to point where you started and knot on the inside of jar. For this reason, you should begin at the back of jar.

5 Stuff the jar well with polyfill. Fill it little by little, pressing the jar out from the inside (especially at the bottom) to achieve the desired shape. Linen is pretty pliable this way. Stuff until you've reached the top and add a nice rounded fluff at the end.

6 Cut a 6" (15.2cm) circle from the square of red gingham. No need to be exact here. Center it over the jar and smooth the fabric down the sides of the jar with a pencil. Starting at the front of the jar (and leaving tails so that you can tie a bow at the end) stitch around the rim of the jar, just beneath the red gingham binding with perle cotton. Make sure these stitches catch the red gingham circle that's running down the sides of the jar to secure it in place. Tug on the tail ends ever so slightly when finished to pull them taught enough to make a slight indentation in the jar, then tie the perle cotton in a knot. Lastly tie a bow.

7 To make the patch, see the instructions at "My Favorite Patch". Embroider a running stitch border with three strands of black floss. Use three strands of black floss to embroider the words "jam xx". Applique the wool felt strawberry with matching colored floss and embroider the strawberry seeds and stem in green floss. Applique the patch by hand to the center of the jam jar.

Charming
Pockets

many pockets house hanging

What a fun way to organize your things! Six charming pockets make this house hanging practical and pretty. I've got one in my sewing room and I've found there is no better place for my little scissors and seam ripper. There's also one hanging in my girls room' ~ the little pockets are perfect for their hair clips and elastics. I hope you enjoy using up some of your little scraps and bits of trim and buttons to decorate your house exactly to your style.

Finished Size
7 ½" x 14"
19 x 35.6 cm

YOU WILL NEED

- Eight rectangles of brown gingham 1 ½" x ¾" (3.8 x 1.9cm) for window frame
- Four rectangles of brown gingham 2 ¾" x ¾" (7 x 1.9cm) for window frame
- Sixteen squares of floral print 1 ½" (3.8cm) for window
- Four squares of cotton solid 3" (7.6cm) for window pocket lining
- Two rectangles of green print 1 ½" x 3" (3.8 x 7.6cm) for house
- Two rectangles of green print 6" x 3" (15.2 x 7.6cm) for house
- One rectangle of green print 6" x 1 ½" (15.2 x 3.8cm) for house
- Two rectangles of green print 1 ½" x 6 ¼" (3.8 x 15.9cm) for house
- One rectangle of green print 8" x 1 ¼" (20.3 x 3.2cm) for house
- One rectangle of green print 8" x 4" (20.3 x 10.2cm) for house
- One rectangle of cotton solid 8" x 10 ½" (20.3 x 26.7cm) for back of window pocket
- Two rectangles of light green dot fabric 8" x 3 ¼" (20.3 x 8.3cm) for bottom pocket
- Two rectangles of green print 8" x 11" (20.3 x 28cm) for house base front and back
- Two rectangles of pink floral print 10" x 4 ¼" (25.4 x 10.8cm) for roof front and back
- One piece of ¾" (1.9cm) width crochet trim 8" (20.3cm) in length for top pocket
- One piece of ½" (1.3cm) width crochet trim 8" (20.3cm) in length for bottom pocket
- One rectangle of fusible interfacing 8" x11" (20.3 x 28cm)
- One rectangle of fusible interfacing 10" x 4 ¼" (25.4 x 10.8cm) for roof
- One rectangle of cotton batting 10" x 4 ¼" (25.4 x 10.8cm) for roof
- One printed cotton label
- One ribbon 4 ½" (11.4cm) in length for hanging loop
- Green embroidery floss (DMC 701)
- Brown embroidery floss (DMC 839)
- Peach embroidery floss (DMC 967)
- Six assorted pink buttons
- Fusible web

INSTRUCTIONS

1 To make windows, sew one piece (a) between two pieces of (c). Repeat until you have sewn eight of these "half windows". Sew one piece (b) between two "half windows". You will have one complete window block (four squares divided by window frame). Press all seams to one side. Repeat until you have four complete window blocks. With right sides facing, sew white lining (d) to one side of a window. Fold the window right sides out, press, and trim off any excess lining.

2 Sew one piece (e) in between two windows, aligning the bottom edges. Press the seams towards piece (e). Repeat with second piece (e) and two remaining windows.

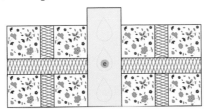

3 Lay one piece of joined windows on top of one piece (f); both should have right sides facing up. Align the bottom edges and machine-baste the bottom edge. Topstitch piece (e) between the two windows. Repeat with the second piece (f) and second piece of joined windows. Trim along the top of both pieces so that they each measure 6" x 2 7/8" (15.2 x 7.3cm).

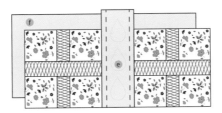

4 With right sides facing, sew piece (g) to the top of one window piece. Press the seam towards piece (g). With right sides facing, align the top raw edge of piece (g) to the bottom edge of the second window piece and sew to attach. Press the seam towards piece (g). Topstitch along the two seams. Square off this piece to 6" x 6 ¼" (15.2 x 15.9cm).

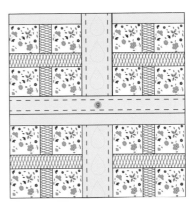

5 With right sides facing, sew piece (h) to one side of the window piece and press the seam towards piece (h). Topstitch. Repeat with second piece (h) on opposite side. It should now measure 8" x 6 ¼" (20.3 x 15.9cm).

6 With right sides facing, sew piece (i) to the top of the window piece. Press the seam towards piece (i) and topstitch the seam. Sew piece (j) to the bottom of the window piece. Press the seam towards piece (j) and topstitch. Machine-baste trim to the top raw edge of piece (i). Sew piece (k), right sides facing to the trim-lined edge of the window piece. Turn right sides out (the crochet trim should now be sticking up) and press. Topstitch that seam.

7 Make bottom pocket. Machine-baste trim to the long side of one piece (l). Pin both pieces (l) right sides together and sew along the trim-lined edge. Turn the pieces right side out and press. (The crochet trim should now be sticking up.) Top stitch a millimeter below the edge. Sew a running stitch with

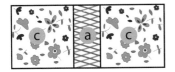

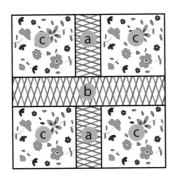

three strands of brown floss a millimeter below the topstitching. Sew the six button "flowers" in place with peach floss and embroider the stems and leaves with three strands of green floss. Pin the bottom pocket to the window piece, aligning the bottom edges, and machine-baste along bottom and sides of pocket.

8 Fuse interfacing to wrong side of one piece (m). Lay out this piece right side up. Lay the pocket piece, right side up on top of this, aligned at bottom. Lay second piece (m) on top of this, wrong side up. Pin together. Sew a ¼" (.6cm) seam along sides and bottom edge, backstitching at beginning and end. Turn right side out. Topstitch, again, below the bottom windows (this adds stability to the bottom pocket and shortens the big pocket behind the windows, giving the entire house more stability.)

9 Fold two pieces (n) in half and cut diagonally to create a triangle 10" (25.4cm) in length and 4 ¼" (10.8cm) tall at the point. Fuse interfacing to the wrong side of one triangle (this will be the back) and cotton batting to the wrong side of the second triangle (this will be the front). Center a cotton label to the right side of the front triangle and stitch to secure. With right sides facing, center the bottom edge of front triangle to the top edge of the house. Sew a ¼" (.6cm) seam. Press the triangle up.

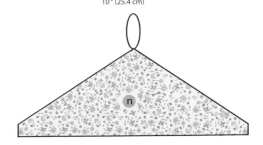

10" (25.4 cm)

4¼" (10.8 cm)

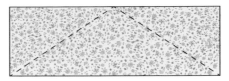

10 Fold the hanging loop in half and sew the raw edges to the point of the back triangle's right side. Pin the triangle back to the triangle front, right sides facing, and sew along the top edges. Turn right side out and press. Clip the pointy corners. Press the raw edge of the back triangle to its underside ¼" (.6cm) and stitch by hand to the backside. Turn the house over and topstitch along the bottom and short sides of roof.

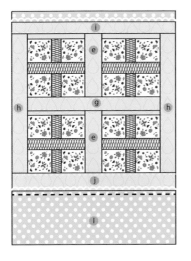

home sweet home embroidery

The color of chocolate is brown ~ deep rich cocoa brown ~ and that is precisely why I love brown so. Chocolate is comforting... just like home, so it was only natural for me to choose chocolate brown for the main color of this embroidery. I added accent colors that would really pop on the natural linen and add just the right amount of color for me. The wonderful thing about embroidery is that you can change the entire look of a design by using your own favorite color palette, or simply using a different color base cloth. But no matter how you stitch it, the sentiment will be the same: Home sweet home!

Finished Size
7" (18cm) circle,
framed in a 9" (23cm) hoop

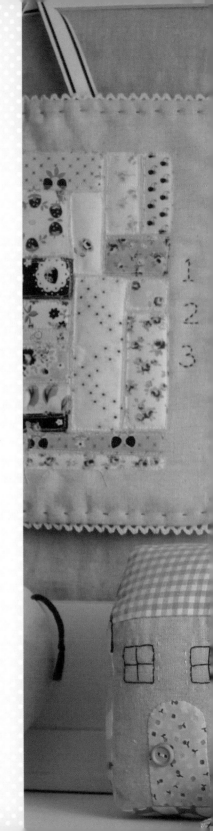

YOU WILL NEED

- One square of linen 12″ x 12″ (30.5 x 30.5cm) for base cloth
- One 9″ (223cm) embroidery hoop
- Home Sweet Home embroidery pattern
- Water-soluble ink pen or pencil

- One skein each of embroidery floss:
    Brown (DMC 898)
    White (DMC 3865)
    Light pink (DMC 963)
    Peach (DMC 353)
    Pink (DMC 761)
    Light lime green (DMC 3348)
    Orange (DMC 922)
    Ice blue (DMC 747)
    Light Periwinkle (DMC 794)
    Silver Metallic (DMC E168)
    Green (DMC 562)
    Coral (DMC 3705)
    Aqua (DMC 964)
    Lavender/pink (DMC 3609)
    Light tan (DMC 738)
    Robin's egg blue (DMC 504)

INSTRUCTIONS

1 Transfer the embroidery design onto linen. Copy the "Home Sweet Home" embroidery pattern onto a piece of paper and tape to a sunny window. Press your linen square and center it over the pattern. Tape securely in place. Trace the pattern onto the linen using a water-soluble ink pen or pencil.

2 Brown: Use three strands to stem stitch the words "home sweet home." Two strands to outline everything in backstitch. One strand to make the cat's whiskers; to make the lines on the book page; to make running stitch lines on the tomato pincushion; and to backstitch the stripes on the sock.

3 White: Use two strands to satin stitch within the scallop border on the house, and on the foot and heel of the sock.

4 Light Pink: Use two strands to satin stitch the stripes on the house roof; to make one French knot beneath each house window; to fill stitch the cupcake frosting; and to make a French knot at the center of the flower on the teacup.

5 Peach: Use two strands to make a French knot beneath each house window.

6 Pink: Use two strands to make two French knots beneath each house window and to satin stitch inside the cat's ears.

7 Light lime green: Use two strands to backstitch the greenery above the house doors. One strand to stitch all the greenery beneath each house window, and the grass at the base of the house.

8 Orange: Use two strands to make a running stitch on the cat's face.

9 Ice blue: Use two strands to fill stitch the cupcake liner and to make the lazy daisy flower on the teacup.

10 Light Periwinkle: Use two strands to fill in the book cover

11 Silver metallic: Use one strand to stem stitch the pins on the tomato pincushion.

12 Green: Use two strands to fill stitch the tomato pincushion leaves.

13 Coral: Use two strands to stitch sprinkles on the cupcake and to satin stitch the pin on the left of the tomato pincushion.

14 Aqua: Use two strands to fill stitch the house doors, and to satin stitch the pin on the right of the tomato pincushion.

15 Lavender/Pink: Use two strands to satin stitch the pin in the middle of the tomato pincushion.

16 Light Tan: Use two strands to fill stitch the cream tea inside the teacup.

17 Robin's egg blue: Use two strands to fill stitch the stripes on the sock.

eyeglasses pouch

Eyeglasses, sunglasses, reading glasses... rotary cutter? Yep, after making this pouch I realized it was not only good for any type of glasses, but my rotary cutter fit inside perfectly too! Well, I'm not worried about my rotary cutter, but I can't tell you how many times I've ruined a pair of glasses by throwing them in my bag along with everything else. A small pouch like this one is too cute not to use! I chose a velcro patch for easy opening and closing but you could just as easily sew in a snap if you prefer. Make one of these fun pouches and your glasses will thank you!

Finished Size
3 ½" x 7"
7.6 x 18 cm

YOU WILL NEED

- Two rectangles of base fabric 4" x 7 ½" (10.2 x 19cm) for front and back
- One ribbon (any width you like) 7 ½" (19cm) in length for front of pouch
- Two rectangles of printed cotton 4" x 7 ½" (10.2 x 19cm) for lining
- Two rectangles of cotton batting 4" x 7 ½" (10.2 x 19cm)
- Two rectangles of mint linen 3 ¼" x 3 ½" (8.3 x 8.9cm) for closure flap
- One square of cotton batting 3" (7.6cm) for flap
- Eyeglass case flap template
- Cardstock, cereal box, or other cardboard
- Velcro patches
- Button

- Patch (linen + interfacing rectangles 2 ¼" x 1 ¾") (5.7 x 4.4cm)
- Black thread
- Brown embroidery floss (DMC 3031)

INSTRUCTIONS

1 Spray-baste the cotton batting to the wrong side of base fabrics, front and back pieces.

2 Use a glue stick or pins to position the long ribbon to the center of pouch front. Sew to attach.

3 Create the closure flap. Use the template to create a pattern, and trace pattern onto the wrong side of linen. Cut a piece of batting using the pattern and spray-baste to linen, within the traced line. Place the second piece of mint linen beneath and sew along the traced line. Cut out the flap, leaving a ¼" (.6cm) seam allowance and clip curves. Turn flap right side out and press. Top stitch ¼" (.6cm) in from the edge.

4 Sew flap to back of pouch piece. With right sides facing, place the back of pouch and closure flap together, aligned at raw edges. Sew a ¼" (.6cm) seam, making sure that the flap does not extend within a ¼" (.6cm) from both sides.

5 Sew the lining pieces to pouch. Lay one lining piece on top of pouch front, right sides facing and sew along top edge. Lay one lining piece on top of pouch back, right sides facing, and sew along top edge. Press open.

6 Pin the closure flap's edges towards center of pouch so that the sides will not get sewn up in the side seams. Pin the pouch's front and back, right sides facing, and the lining pieces, right sides facing. Pin well at center seam. Sew along all four edges, leaving a 2" (5cm) opening in the side of lining for turning right side out. Turn pouch and lining right side out and sew the opening closed by hand. Ease out all the corners and tuck the lining inside pouch. Press the closure flap into its proper place.

7 To make the patch, see the instructions at "My Favorite Patch". Embroider a running stitch border with three strands of brown floss. Use two strands of black thread to embroider the words "100% Cotton" or whatever words you choose. Applique the patch by hand to the center of pouch, centered over the ribbon.

8 Sew a button to the front of the closure flap. Sew Velcro to pouch and under the closure flap by hand.

airmail simple tote

I love mail. The good kind, you know ~ not the bills, but the handwritten letters and surprise packages from friends who live across the globe, or even just across town. I keep an old cigar box filled with pretty letters and pretty stamps and I love to go through them occasionally. And since I know I'm not alone on the airmail-love, I designed this simple tote bag with a fun "airmail" envelope pocket on the front. Because who doesn't love good mail? And who couldn't use another tote?

Finished Size
12" x 14" x 3"
30.4 x 35.6 x 7.6 cm

YOU WILL NEED

- One rectangle of cotton print 9" x 4 ½" (22.9 x 11.4cm) for envelope flap
- One rectangle of white solid cotton 9" x 4 ½" (22.9 x 11.4cm) for envelope flap lining
- One rectangle of cotton print 9 ½" x 5 ½" (24.1 x 14cm) for envelope pocket
- One rectangle of white solid cotton 9 ½" x 5 ½" (24.1 x 14cm) for envelope pocket lining
- Two rectangles of horizontal stripe fabric 16" x 14" (40.6 x 35.6cm) for bag exterior
- Two rectangles of vertical stripe fabric 16" x 3 ¼" (40.6 x 8.3cm) for exterior top of bag
- Two strips of accent fabric 16" x 1" (40.6 x 2.5cm) for bag exterior accent
- Two cotton webbing handles 19" (48cm) in length each (38" total) (97cm)
- Two rectangles of pre-quilted fabric 16" x 16 ¾" (40.6 x 42.5cm) for bag lining
- One piece of crochet trim 12 ½" (32cm) in length
- One ribbon 1 ¾" (4.4cm) in length for tab at side of envelope
- One piece of printed cotton ribbon (any size) for envelope flap
- One button
- Dark lime green embroidery floss (DMC 581)
- Pistachio green embroidery floss (DMC 3817)
- Fusible web

- Patch (linen + interfacing rectangles 3" x 2 ¼") (7.6 x 5.7cm)
- Black thread
- Silver metallic embroidery floss (DMC E168)

INSTRUCTIONS

1 Cut the envelope flap and its backing fabric as shown (insert pic). Then trace a   at the pointy part of the envelope flap pieces and trim. Attach crochet trim to the V-line on the right side of the envelope flap fabric, folding back the raw edges at each end of the crochet trim for a clean finish.

2 Make the button loop. Cut three 9" (23cm) pieces of the dark lime green embroidery floss. Tie in a knot at one end and pin the knot to something secure so you can braid it. Braid the three strands until you have a 2" (5cm) length of braid. Knot tightly. Sew the braided loop to the rounded point of the envelope flap, making sure both knots are below the ¼" (.6cm) stitch line, and the loop is laying against the right side of fabric.

3 Pin the envelope flap front and lining pieces together, right sides facing. Sew along all sides, leaving a 2" (5cm) opening at the top of the flap for turning right side out. Turn right side out, ease out all corners and press. Press a piece of printed cotton ribbon, backed with fusible web, to the center of the envelope flap and stitch in place. Set aside.

4 Add a ribbon tab to the lower left hand side of the envelope pocket, if you like. Fold the ribbon in half and align the raw edges to the raw edge of the envelope pocket fabric. Machine-baste in place. With right sides facing, sew the envelope pocket front and lining pieces together, leaving a 2" (5cm) opening along the bottom of the envelope for turning right side out. Turn right side out,

ease out all the corners and press well. Set aside.

5 To assemble the bag exterior, repeat the following steps for both front and back of bag: Press a strip of accent fabric in half lengthwise. Sew the folded strip of accent fabric to the top edge of the horizontal stripes (right sides facing and raw edges aligned). Pin the vertical stripes fabric to the same edge (right sides facing and raw edges aligned) and sew a ¼" (.6cm) seam. Press the seam towards the vertical stripes.

6 Sew the envelope to the front of bag: The envelope flap is centered on the bag front, and located 2 ½" (6.4cm) below the accent trim. Pin in place and topstitch along the top straight

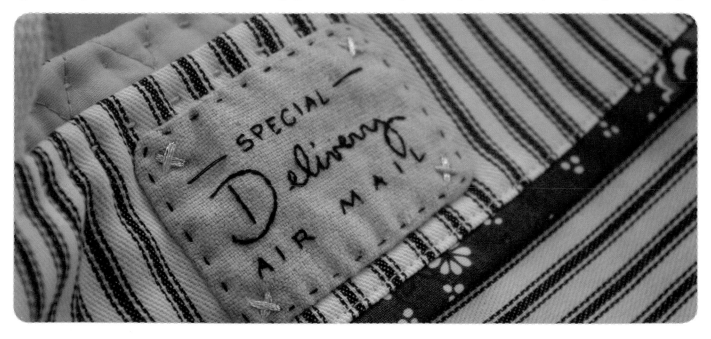

edge of envelope flap only. The envelope pocket piece is located approximately 1" (2.5cm) below the top of the envelope flap and centered. Pin in place and top-stitch the envelope pocket along the sides and bottom edge. To determine where to sew your button on the envelope pocket, mark a dot through the button loop. Sew the button in place.

7 Attach handles. One handle should be pinned to the bag front and one to the bag back ~ centered, with the ends spaced 5" (12.7cm) apart. Pin the handles, raw edges aligned with the top of the bag and with the U-shape laying against the right side of the fabric. Machine-baste the handles in place.

8 With right sides facing, pin one quilted lining piece to the bag front and one quilted lining piece to the bag back. Sew a ½" (1.3cm) seam across the top edges. Press open and pin these pieces together, right sides facing ~ bag front to bag back, and lining to lining. Pin especially well at the seam where bag and lining meet. Sew a ¼" (.6cm) seam around all four raw sides, leaving a 3" (8cm) opening for turning along one side of the lining. Before turning, fold all four corners of the bag into triangles and mark a 3" (7.6cm) line across each (the line should run 1 ½" (3.8cm) equally on either side of the center seam of these triangles). Stitch across your marked lines (I always stitch along the line twice to reinforce the seam). Turn the bag right side out and stitch the

opening closed by hand. Smooth the lining into the bag.

9 You may optionally sew a running stitch along the top edge of the bag with six strands of floss and a strong sharp needle (I used pistachio green DMC 3817).

10 To make the patch, see the instructions at "My Favorite Patch". Embroider a running stitch border with two strands of black thread. Use two strands of black thread to embroider the words "Special Delivery, AIRMAIL" and six strands of silver floss to embroider small x's in each corner. Applique the patch by hand to the front of bag, centered in the vertical stripe section.

simple zipper patchwork pouch

Sweet and simple, this easy zipper patchwork pouch is one of my favorite things to make. Arranging the patchwork is the part I like best. This pouch makes use of those tiny scraps in your favorite prints that you just couldn't bear to throw away. And who couldn't use a sweet patchwork pouch to hold quarters or candy or stamps? Or buttons or love notes, or tickets, or rocks? There are a million and one reasons you need a new pouch ~ let's get started!

Finished Size
6" x 4 ½"
15.2 x 11.4 cm

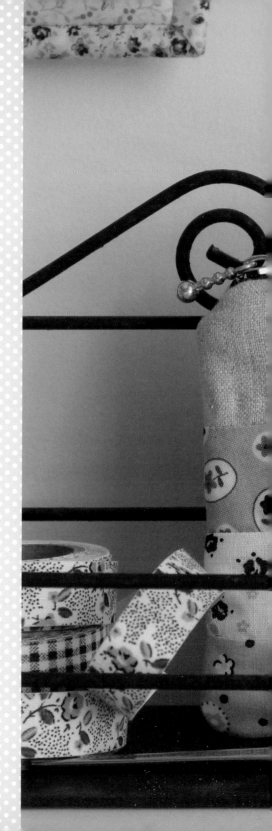

LINEN + COTTON
handmade

YOU WILL NEED

- Thirty-six squares of assorted cotton prints 1 ½" (3.8cm) for patchwork front and back
- Two rectangles of linen 7" x 2" (17.8 x 5cm) for front and back
- Two squares of linen 1 ½" (3.8cm) for zipper tabs
- Two rectangles of lining fabric 6 ¾" x 5" (17.1 x 12.7cm)
- Two rectangles of cotton batting 6 ¾" x 5" (17.1 x 12.7cm)
- One zipper 7" (17.8cm)
- Thread spool for tracing
- Zipper foot attachment
- Pale pink embroidery floss (DMC 818)

- Patch (linen + interfacing rectangles 3" x 2") (7.6 x 5cm)
- Black thread
- Brown embroidery floss (DMC 3031)
- Ecru embroidery floss (DMC Ecru)

INSTRUCTIONS

1 To make the patchwork for the front, arrange your 1 ½" (3.8cm) squares in a pleasing arrangement of three rows of six squares. Sew the first row together, pressing the seams to the right, sew the middle row and press seams to the left, then sew the bottom row and press seams to the right again. This way, when you're sewing the rows together, the seams will butt against one another and match up more easily. Repeat these steps to make another set of patchwork for the back of pouch.

2 Place patchwork front and linen rectangle together, right sides facing, aligned at the top. Sew ¼" (.6cm) seam. Repeat for back of pouch. Press the seam towards the patchwork.

3 Spray-baste batting to the wrong side of patchwork pieces. Quilt, if you like. I embroidered a running stitch across the linen with three strands of pale pink embroidery floss, ¼" (.6cm) above the patchwork seam.

4 Using a large spool of thread, trace a curved edge at the bottom corners of the patchwork and cut carefully along your traced line. Do this for both front and back patchwork pieces, as well as the bottom corners of both lining pieces.

5 To add the zipper tabs, place a 1 ½" (3.8cm) square of linen on top of the zipper, aligned at the end. Sew across the linen and zipper where the zipper ends. Finger press the linen back. Trim excess linen. Repeat at the beginning end of the zipper.

6 To sew the zipper, lay a lining piece right side up, the zipper (aligned at the top of lining piece) also right side up, and the patchwork front, right side down.) Using your zipper foot, sew across the top, creating a ¼" (.6cm) seam, backstitching at both ends. Press the lining and front piece away from the zipper. Repeat on other side.

7 Unzip the zipper about halfway and pin the lining pieces together, right sides facing. Pin the front and back patchwork pieces right sides together. Push the zipper in towards the patchwork side. Sew around all four edges, leaving a 2" (5cm) opening in the side of the lining, for turning right side out.

8 Turn right side out, easing out the corners. Press well. Handstitch the opening in the lining closed, and then tuck the lining into the pouch.

9 To make the patch, see the instructions at "My Favorite Patch." Embroider a running stitch border with three strands of brown floss. Use two strands of black thread to embroider the words "LINEN + COTTON handmade," and also to backstitch the greenery. Use 6 strands of ecru floss to make three French knots. Applique the patch by hand to the upper half of the two center patchwork squares on the front of the pouch.

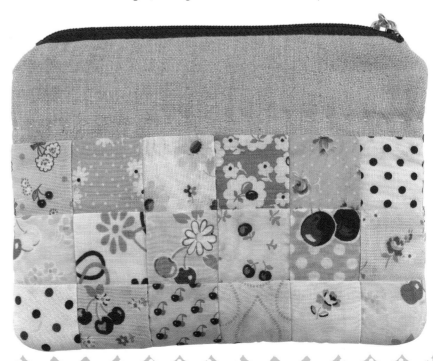

starburst dresden plate pillow

I love the effect a simple triangle insert makes on a traditional Dresden plate. I also love working with cotton lawn ~ it's fine and soft and feels nearly weightless. Of course, any fabric will work just fine and the color palette is up to you. Complete the look with a few running stitches in multi-colored floss to accentuate the shape of your Dresden plate. This is a delightfully quick project and the best part comes when you're all finished ~ place a pillow insert inside, jump on the couch, and snuggle up with your newest handmade masterpiece!

Finished Size
20" x 20"
50.8 x 50.8 cm

YOU WILL NEED

- 10 rectangles of assorted cotton lawn prints measuring at least 6" x 8" (15.2 x 20.3cm) for cutting two Dresden plate petals
- One strip of white cotton lawn at least 42" x 5" (107 x 12.7cm) for cutting twenty triangle inserts
- One square of neutral print fabric 4 ¾" (12cm) for Dresden center circle
- One square of lightweight interfacing (NOT fusible)
- One square of linen 20 ½" (52cm) for pillow base
- One rectangle of linen 20 ½" x 10" for (52 x 25.4cm) pillow back
- One rectangle of linen 20 ½" x 13 ½" (52 x 34.2cm) for pillow back
- Two pieces of pre-made single fold binding totaling 42" (107cm) or two strips of cotton lawn print 20 ½" x 1 ½" (52 x 3.8cm) to make your own pillow back binding
- Starburst Dresden templates
- Cardstock, cereal box or other thin cardboard to make patterns
- Pearl Cotton Variations thread in reds to purples (DMC 4211)
- Pearl Cotton Variations thread in greens to blues (DMC 4030)

- Patch (linen + interfacing rectangles 2 ¼" x 2 ¼") (5.7 x 5.7cm)
- Black thread
- Brown embroidery floss (DMC 3031)

INSTRUCTIONS

1 Make patterns from the templates using sturdy cardboard, as these patterns will be traced many times while making this pillow.

2 The Dresden plate is composed of twenty petals and I have made my plate with ten different prints ~ two petals x each print = twenty petals. From the ten rectangles of cotton lawn, trace and cut two petals. Fold the longer straight edge at the top of each petal in half, right sides facing, and sew a ¼" (.6cm) seam across. Turn the point of that seam right side out and press your petal's new triangular tip. Repeat for twenty petals. Lay them out in the arrangement you would like for your Dresden plate.

3 From the 5" (12.7cm) strip of white cotton lawn, cut 20 triangle inserts. To avoid having to perfectly fold such small pieces of fabric, I have drawn the pattern in half, requiring you to place the pattern on a folded piece of fabric. My suggestion is to start from one side of the 42" x 5" (107 x 12.7cm) piece and press a fold of 1" (2.5cm); place the pattern on the fold and cut directly along the long angled side with your rotary cutter. Fold that edge over 1" (2.5cm) and cut. Continue until you have 20. The narrowest end of the triangle must measure slightly less than ¼" (.6cm) ~ if yours measures more than this, please trim your pattern piece and start over.

4 Sew the petals and inserts together. As with a traditional Dresden plate assembly, you will begin sewing two petals together, right sides facing, up near the finished end of the petals. Begin by backstitching a centimeter up to the finished edge, then continuing back down the sides to the narrow part of the petals. However, for this plate, you will first insert a white triangle between the petal edges, as shown. (The wider edge of triangle is placed down with the narrow ends of the petals; the long raw edge of the triangle is aligned with the petals' side edges.) For best accuracy, use a dab of glue stick to secure the triangle between two petals. Sew the petals as usual. Sew the petals together, adding one at a time and press all seams to the same side. Continue until all 20 petals have been sewn and the plate is complete. Press well.

5 Trace the Dresden Plate Center Circle pattern to the wrong side of center fabric. Place the square of light-weight interfacing beneath this and sew around the traced line. Trim a ¼" (.6cm) seam allowance around the sewn line and cut a slit in the center of the interfacing with a seam ripper. Turn the circle right side out and press. Applique by hand to the center of your Dresden plate.

6 Applique the Dresden plate by hand or machine to your linen square as desired. I centered mine, but it might be fun to place it off center as well. Then stitch the white "starbursts" by hand or machine, if desired.

7 Using the Pearl Cotton Variations thread I embroidered small x's around half the circle at the center of my Dresden plate. I also embroidered two running stitch borders around the Dresden plate (first in greens and blues, second in reds and purples.)

8 To make the pillow back, attach the single fold binding to one long edge of both pieces of linen for pillow back. If you are making your own, press the two strips of cotton lawn in half lengthwise. Then press each raw edge in towards the center crease and press again. Attach to both linen pillow back pieces.

9 With right sides facing, pin the 20 ½" x 10" (52 x 25.4cm) pillow backing piece to the pillow front, raw edges aligned at the top. Pin the 20 ½" x 13 ½" (52 x 34.2cm) pillow backing piece onto the pillow, raw edges aligned at the bottom. When using linen, pin well. Sew along all four edges of the pillow, backstitching over the sides where the backing pieces overlap. Zig-zag stitch over the raw edges on all four sides. Turn pillow right side out.

10 To make the patch, see the instructions at "My Favorite Patch". Embroider a running stitch border with three strands of brown floss. Use two strands of black thread to embroider the words "100% linen xx". Applique the patch by hand to the lower right corner.

PATTERNS

"Mouse House" Doll Quilt
Page 44

Sweet dreams
Sleep tight
I love you
Goodnight!

ABC Tote Bag

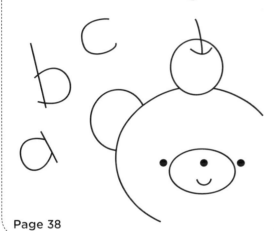

Page 38

On The Spot Trivet
Page 56

Bon
cáfe

Simple Zipper Patchwork Pouch
Page 104

LINEN + COTTON
handmade

Airmail Simple Tote
Page 98

─ SPECIAL ─
Delivery
A I R   M A I L

Jam Jar Pin Cushion
Page 78

YUM!   Jam

Baby Bear Rattle
Page 14

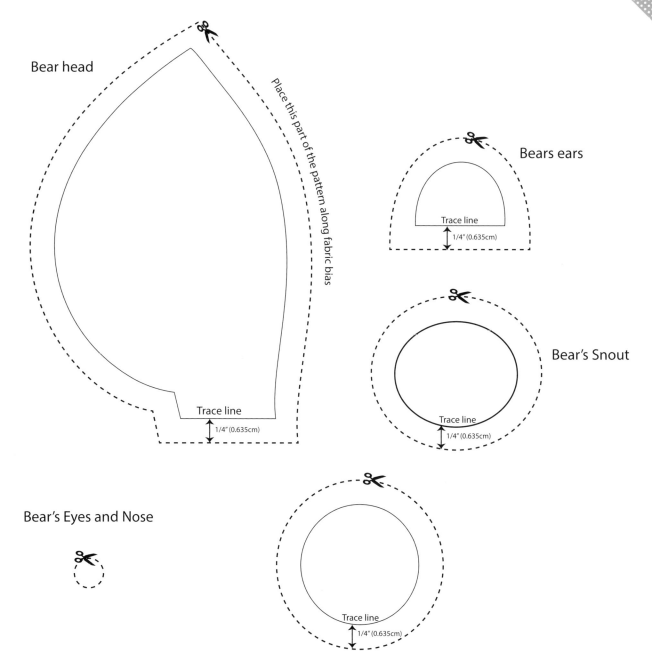

Bear head

Place this part of the pattern along fabric bias

Trace line

1/4" (0.635cm)

Bears ears

Trace line

1/4" (0.635cm)

Bear's Snout

Trace line

1/4" (0.635cm)

Bear's Eyes and Nose

Trace line

1/4" (0.635cm)

Modern Color Block Quilt
Page 20

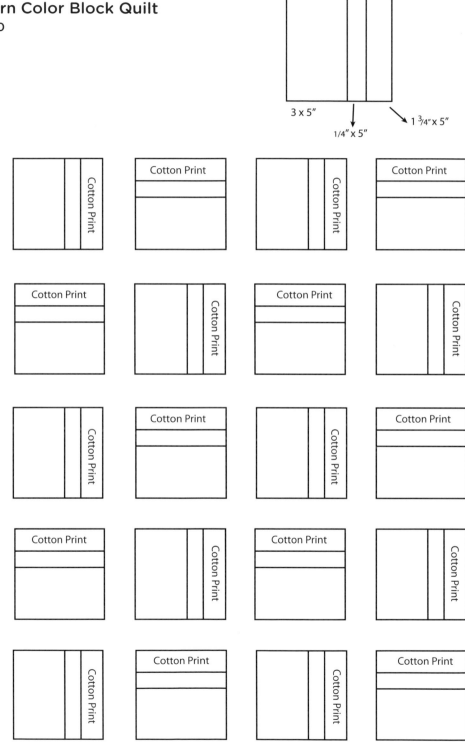

3 x 5"

1/4" x 5"

1 3/4" x 5"

Cotton Print

Cotton Print

Cotton Print

Cotton Print

Cotton Print

Cotton Print

Cotton Print

Cotton Print

Cotton Print

Cotton Print

Cotton Print

Cotton Print

Cotton Print

Cotton Print

Cotton Print

Cotton Print

Cotton Print

Cotton Print

Cotton Print

Cotton Print

Ruffle Collar Bib
Page 26

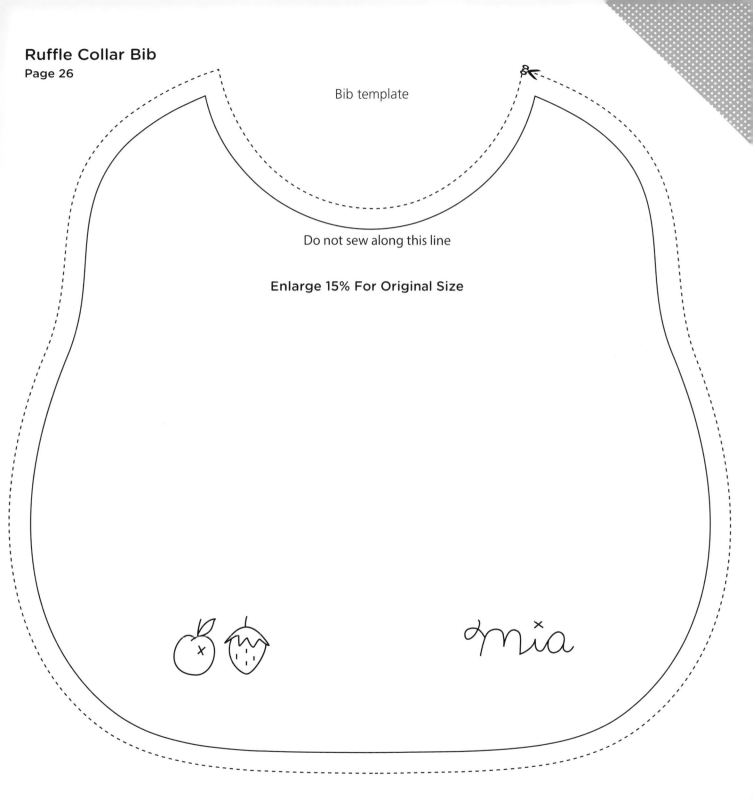

Bib template

Do not sew along this line

Enlarge 15% For Original Size

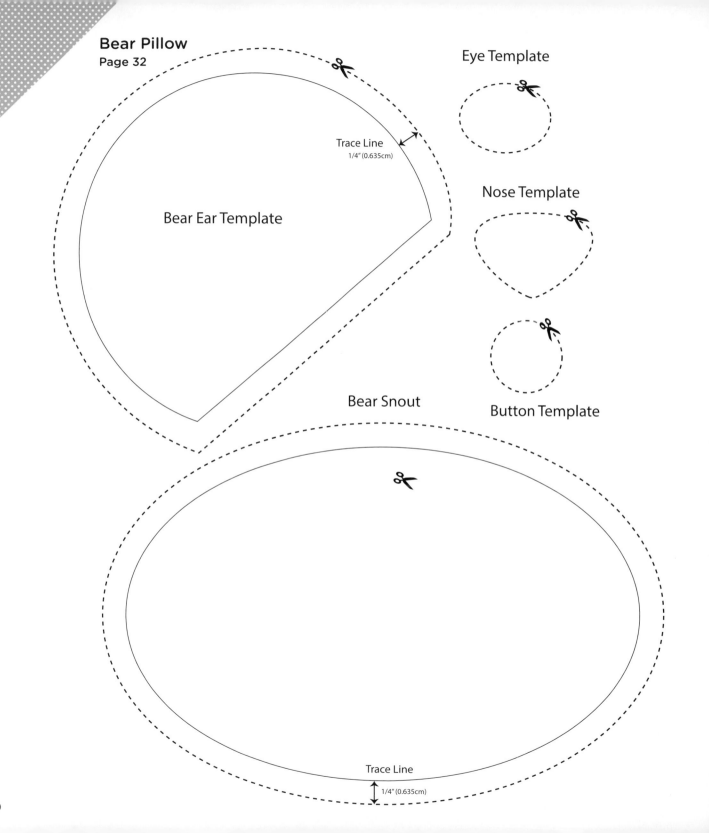

Bear Pillow
Page 32

Eye Template

Trace Line
1/4" (0.635cm)

Bear Ear Template

Nose Template

Bear Snout

Button Template

Trace Line

1/4" (0.635cm)

"Mouse House" Doll Quilt

Page 44

1
Roof
Block
2
Mouse
Print
Block
3
4
5
6

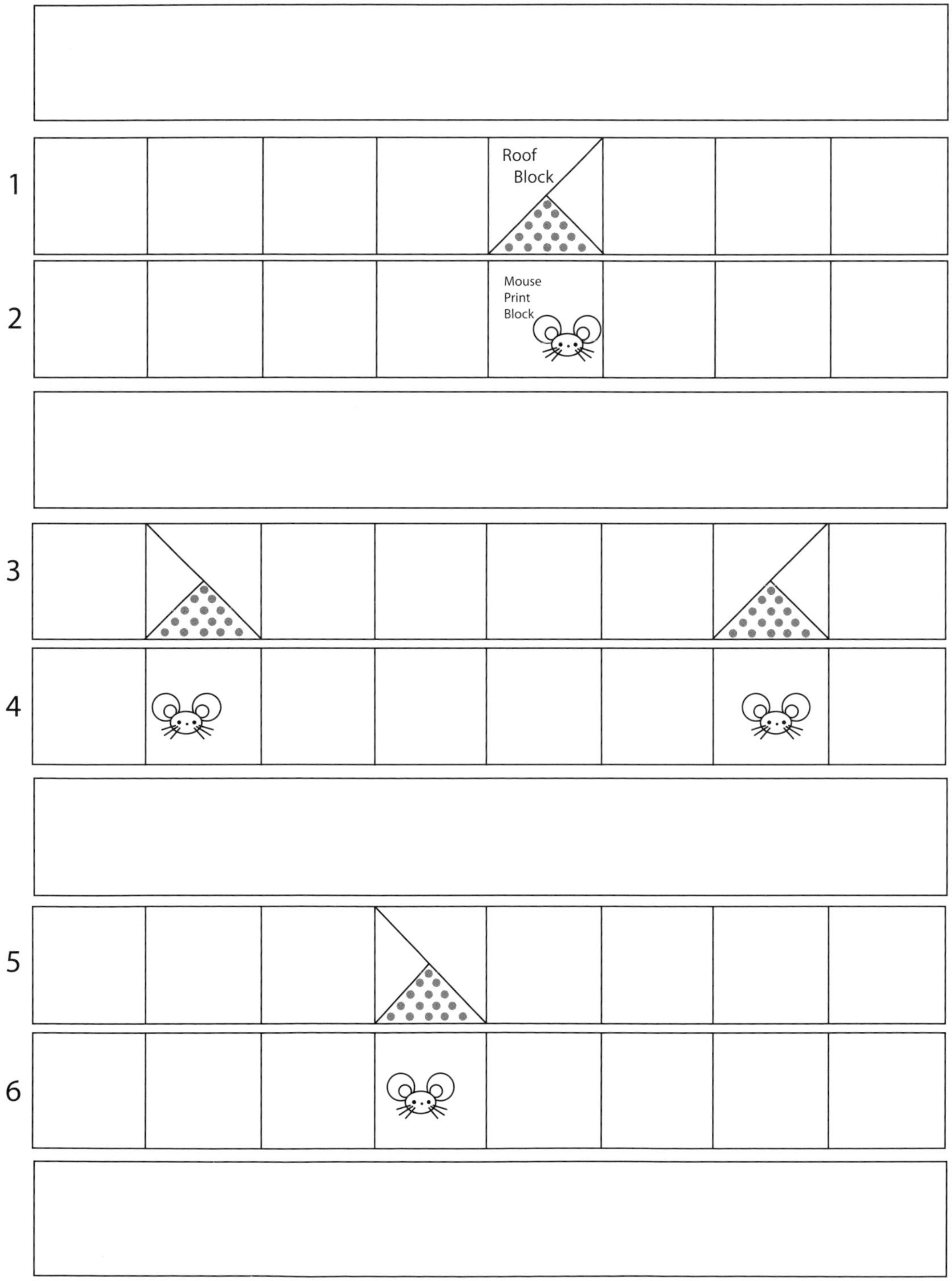

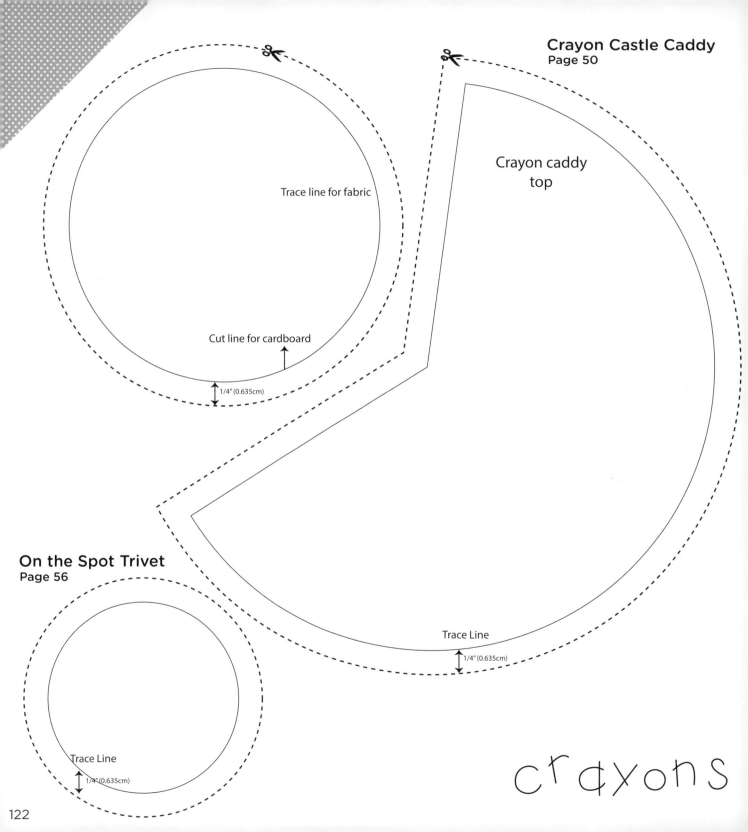

Crayon Castle Caddy
Page 50

Trace line for fabric

Crayon caddy
top

Cut line for cardboard

1/4" (0.635cm)

On the Spot Trivet
Page 56

Trace Line

1/4" (0.635cm)

Trace Line

1/4" (0.635cm)

crayons

Stacked Hexagon Mug Rug

Page 62

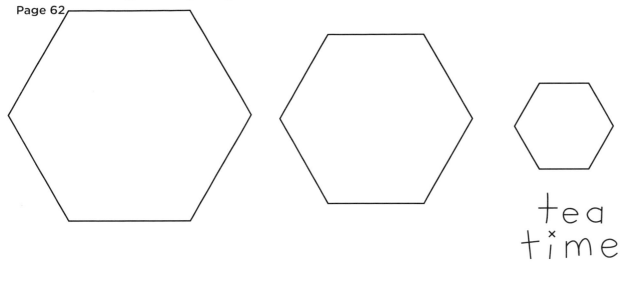

tea
time

Ric-Rac Coasters

Page 68

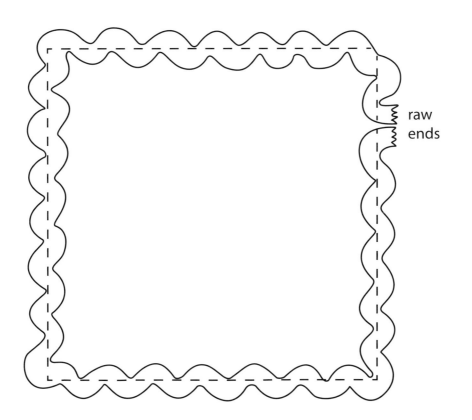

raw
ends

Small Things Fabric Boxes
Page 72

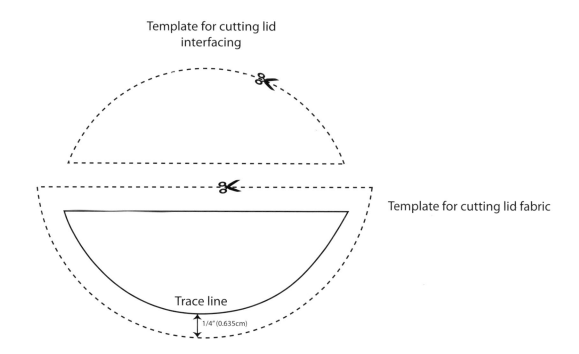

Template for cutting lid
interfacing

Template for cutting lid fabric

Trace line

1/4" (0.635cm)

Many Pockets House Hanging
Page 84

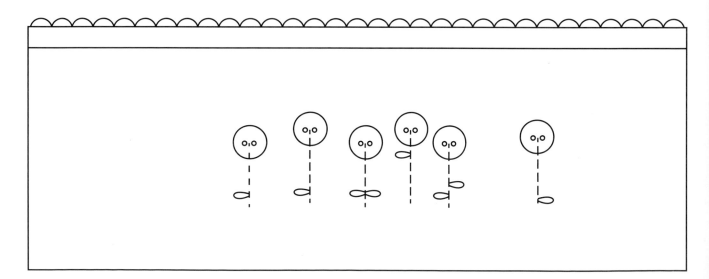

Eyeglasses Pouch
Page 94

100% Cotton

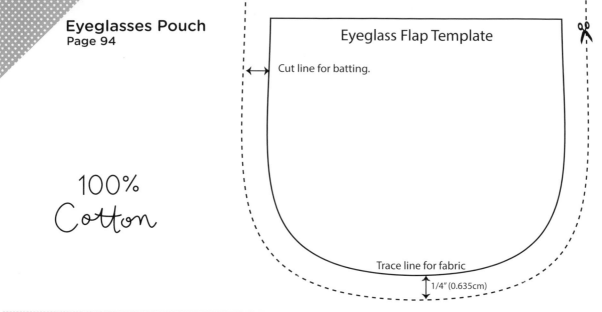

Eyeglass Flap Template

Cut line for batting.

Trace line for fabric

1/4" (0.635cm)

Jam Jar Pin Cushion
Page 78

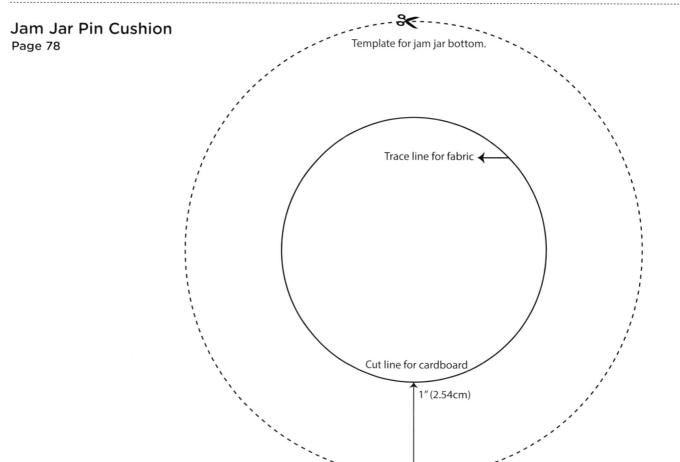

Template for jam jar bottom.

Trace line for fabric

Cut line for cardboard

1" (2.54cm)

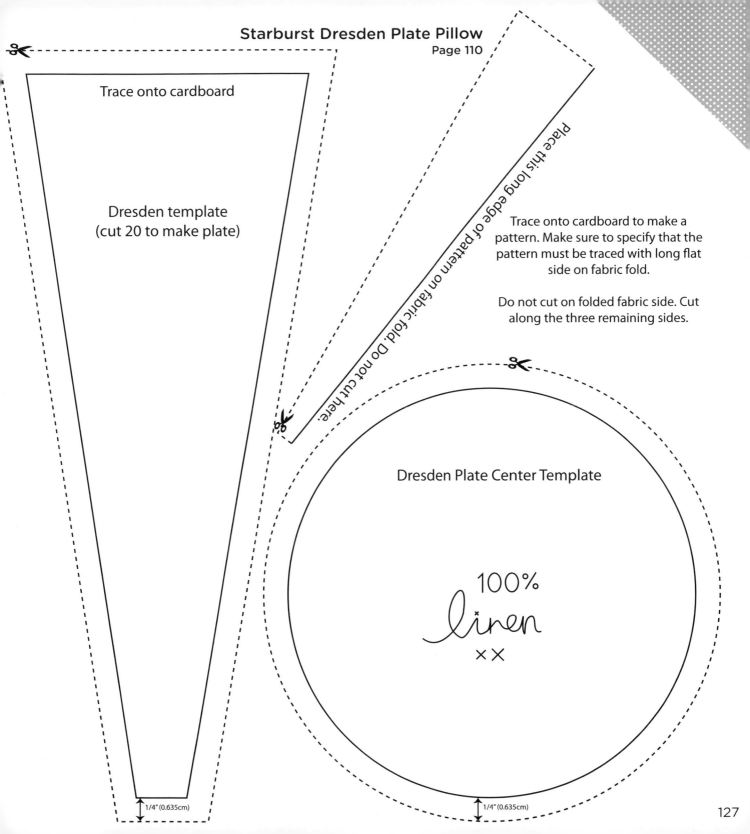

Trace onto cardboard

Dresden template
(cut 20 to make plate)

Place this long edge of pattern on fabric fold. Do not cut here.

Trace onto cardboard to make a pattern. Make sure to specify that the pattern must be traced with long flat side on fabric fold.

Do not cut on folded fabric side. Cut along the three remaining sides.

Dresden Plate Center Template

100%
linen
xx

1/4" (0.635cm)

1/4" (0.635cm)

sources

For embroidery floss:
DMC ~ www.dmc.com

For natural linen:
Jo-Ann Fabric and Craft Stores ~ www.joann.com
Etsy ~ www.etsy.com

For beautiful quilting cotton prints:
Fat Quarter Shop ~ www.fatquartershop.com
Superbuzzy ~ www.superbuzzy.com
Sew Deerly Loved ~ www.etsy.com/shop/sewdeerlyloved
Simply Sweet Fabric ~ www.etsy.com/shop/simplysweetfabric

For crochet lace trims, ribbons and buttons:
Etsy ~ www.etsy.com

For printed cotton tapes and ribbon:
Billy Cotton Shop ~ www.etsy.com/shop/billycottonshop0413

For jingle balls and rattles and other toy inserts:
American Felt & Craft ~ www.feltandcraft.com

For Sulky Sticky Fabri-Solvy:
Amazon ~ www.amazon.com

For Mountain Mist Cream Rose 100% Cotton batting:
Beverly's ~ www.beverlys.com

For Insul-Bright insulated lining:
Amazon ~ www.amazon.com

For Dritz Fabric Glue Stick:
Amazon ~ www.amazon.com

For June Tailor Quilt Basting Spray:
Amazon ~ www.amazon.com